Starting Out
LIFE LESSONS FOR GRADUATES

EDITED BY BECKI SMITH

Islandport Press
P.O. Box 10
Yarmouth, ME 04096

Islandportpress.com
books@islandportpress.com

Copyright 2014 © by Elisabeth D. Smith
All Rights Reserved.

ISBN: 978-1-934031-96-4
Library of Congress Control Number: 2013922643

Dean L. Lunt: Publisher
Cover and book design: Karen Hoots, Hoots Design
Author Photo: R. Jameson Smith
Printed in USA by Versa Press

 *Starting Out*
LIFE LESSONS FOR GRADUATES

For Jake and Maia

Foreword

IN MAY OF 2011, I graduated from NYU's Tisch School of the Arts with a degree in Film and Television. After the commencement at Yankee Stadium, my family celebrated with a wonderful lunch at a restaurant in Central Park. Graduation presents made their way around the table: money, thoughtful cards, and one meticulously wrapped package. It was a book from my mother—and it was no ordinary book.

For months before my graduation, my mother had reached out to a wide range of people, asking them to share a bit of advice for me as I left college and entered "the real world." She had managed to get U.S. senators, filmmakers, writers, comedians, actors, scholars, entrepreneurs, artists, friends, and family to contribute. She named the book "Dust Never Settles: And Other Truths." It was the single greatest gift I have ever received. It is, more or less, the book you hold in your hand.

I was deeply moved. I enthusiastically believe, as many sons do, that I have the best parents in the world. They always believed in me, took chances for me, and made sacrifices for me. They made sure that I had the opportunity to achieve whatever I set my heart on. There comes a time, though, when you feel you no longer need your parents' advice and guidance—you're an adult after all, finished with college, degree in hand. But the truth is graduating can set you adrift. Your daily structure changes drastically, your friends move on, and finding work in today's market is very difficult. I can't say that I felt alone or adrift on that graduation day, but my mother's gift meant the world to me because it made it clear that it was still OK to seek advice, OK if I didn't have all the answers yet. Most important was the unspoken message: my parents were still there for me when I needed them.

After two years in "the real world" pursuing a career as a producer and director in the film industry, I have been fortunate to achieve many of my professional goals—and now I have a little advice to share.

1. HAVE PATIENCE. Members of my generation are hungry for success and accolades. The reality is that in the first years out of school you will likely work harder than anyone else and for very little money. Pay your dues and be patient.

2. HARD WORK NEVER GOES UNNOTICED. Take your time, grow with your peers, earn your successes, take responsibility for your choices, and always be grateful to the people who push and challenge you.

3. TAKE CARE OF YOUR FRIENDS AND MAKE NEW ONES. You never know which of your peers will achieve success first. The goal should be to help each other out and up. In the end you will need friends to console you during setbacks and to celebrate successes. Most of all, people remember when you take care of them and never forget when you don't.

Finally, I'd like to thank my mother—simply, for everything. I am truly grateful she never let the dust settle around me—and I sincerely hope it never does.

—R. JAMESON SMITH (JAKE)
Director | Producer at Park Bench Pictures

Introduction

COMMENCEMENT. One part of your life has ended and another is about to begin. Congratulations; you've graduated! You have a clean slate on which to write the story of the rest of your life. Whoever gave you the gift of this book is proud of you—and so am I.

But starting out can be as scary as it is exhilarating. The freedom to pursue your dreams carries with it the fear that you might not succeed. And it is often fear of success—not fear of failure—that keeps people from achieving their goals.

I have been a television producer for most of my life. As the executive producer of two successful newsmagazine shows, my work has afforded me the opportunity to meet many remarkable people—politicians, authors, actors, musicians, athletes, comedians, and entrepreneurs. I was always touched by their stories, each one individual and interesting. I developed long-term relationships with many of them, and am fortunate to call them friends.

So when my son Jake was, like you, graduating from college and about to start out on his own, I called on my friends and colleagues and asked them to share some of the wisdom they had gleaned along their paths to success. Almost all of them were glad to do so. I gathered their letters to give to Jake as a graduation gift, the genesis for the book you are reading now. Some of these entries are witty, some are biographical, and some are calls to action. All are heartfelt and thoughtful notes, given generously, to share mistakes and triumphs that might help to make your stride to success a little easier.

As Jake writes in the foreword to this volume, he loved the book that these pieces of wisdom became. Others loved the book as well, including his friends, who would pore over the pages. Those who contributed were amazed to see the final work, and those who saw it for the first time would comment that the book should be shared with others. Thus, this very personal gift created for my graduate has now become a book I am sharing with you.

My advice to Jake, to the college students I teach, and to you as you start out, is inspired by Robert Kennedy, who quoted Aeschylus when saying, "Make gentle the life of this world." It's a simple phrase, but in the hurried pace of life, it's not so simple to practice. Life can be tough, and the instinctive response is to be tough right back. Don't. Instead be strong . . . and kind. Be kinder than necessary. By doing so, you will indeed make gentle the life of this world—and yours, as well.

Today, your family and friends are very, very proud of you, and excited for all you are about to be. But know that no one achieves success alone. So, to the graduate who receives this book as a gift, may the wise words of my friends guide you, uplift you, comfort you, and inspire you. Learn from them, lean on them, and, most of all, appreciate them. And then go forward and be like them: authentic and accomplished, sincere and successful, funny and famous, generous and gifted, committed and caring, loyal and loving.

It's your turn now . . . Start out!

BECKI SMITH
former executive producer, WCSH6, teacher

Brian P. Allen, *artistic director, Good Theater*

OVER THE YEARS, I've learned a lot about what I do, and I continue to learn something new every day. Just when you think you've got it all figured out, something will surprise you with a whole new perspective. Be open to that.

One lesson I learned early on was that accepting a job because of the money was the worst reason to take a project. I have to love the project and not just the paycheck. Every time—and I've done it twice—that I took a job because of money, the show was always painful, and an unhappy experience. Some of the shows I've done didn't pay much, but they were pieces that I had to do. These turned out to be some of the greatest theatrical experiences of my life. It is art. It is a living creation. It is not just a quick buck.

I've also learned to trust my own vision. When others are telling you no, but in your gut, something is telling you yes—listen to that. Fight for that. Your gut doesn't lie to you.

Most of all, enjoy the process. The journey should be as much fun as the end result.

Go far, dream big.

◎ ◎ ◎

Amy Bouchard, *founder / owner Isamax Snacks*

HERE IS MY STORY: I have always been a very independent person. . . not really having a choice. I don't have a relationship with my biological father, and my mother left my brother and me for a while when we were younger because she needed to find herself. I have been taking care of myself and working since I was twelve. When I was a junior in High School I announced that I was going to get married to a person I had been dating for about a year (who was away in the Army). I don't think I had seen him for about six months (and I wasn't pregnant) so really there was no reason for me to marry—but I was young and it was what I wanted to do. When he came home I realized that I didn't think I loved him and I was not ready to marry him. We were not getting along. My mother told me: "You will go to marriage counseling before you call off this wedding. There are a lot of people coming and you don't want to disappoint them. "So, I got married. Two weeks later, my new husband left for Germany, I stayed behind to finish school. One week after he left for Germany, he was injured and I had to drop out of school and go to Germany to take care of him. The Army didn't have a place for me to stay. I had to rent an apartment and live there for a month. It was 1985 and not a good time for Americans to be overseas. I was all alone, always getting lost, didn't speak German, and could tell I was not welcome in most of the shops I went in. (I cannot begin to tell you how much I appreciate that awful experience). A month later Jim, my husband, got out of the hospital and we returned to the United States. We stayed in Washington DC for a few weeks, then we went back home to Maine. A year and a half went by. I became a mother. I was nineteen years old, married to a very abusive person, a new mom, and had no High School Diploma. I thought to myself, "What am I going to do?" The odds were against me but I told myself: "I'm going to move forward and not feel sorry for myself."

MISTAKES ARE WONDERFUL THINGS... THEY MAKE YOU SMARTER, WISER, AND ABLE TO APPRECIATE THE SMOOTHER TIMES.

This was the beginning of treating my personal life like a business. I went to night school to finish my education so I could get a job and plan for my life as a single mom. When I got my first good paying job it was at Bath Iron Works. I thought I had died and gone to heaven!! I remember I was so scared working in an office surrounded by people who worked on computers and walked like zombies—they didn't seem very happy. But I was happy. I was a single mother, receiving no child support, yet my son and I had our own apartment and I was making $6.23 an hour. WHOOPIE! I was the lowest paid person at BIW, but probably the happiest! I would bake brownies, cookies, and whoopie pies and bring them to work. I loved how it made everyone happy; plus, I loved the way it made me feel—like I was giving everyone a present. I wanted to bottle up that feeling. That was the place where I began to expand on what makes me happy and turn it into a business to make other people happy. If I can do it anyone can!!

The best advice I could give you is if it feels right; if it makes you have butterflies in your stomach; if it just makes you happy when you think about it, then go with those feelings!! Some of the most successful decisions I have ever made were the opposite of the ones taught in business school. (Remember, I had no business experience). I think you have to go through the bad to get to the good in life. Mistakes are a wonderful things . . . they make you smarter, wiser, and able to appreciate the smoother times.

My last piece of advice? If you are having a bad day or even a good cry . . . look in the mirror before the end of the day and smile. It may be hard to do and, yes, you will look crazy (especially if you have a red puffy face) but I guarantee it will make you feel better.

◎ ◎ ◎

Barry MILLS, *president, Bowdoin College*

MY ADVICE IS TO BE ENTHUSIASTIC, be fearless, and be the best-prepared person in the room. People love to work and be around people who are enthusiastic about what they do. You will face many opportunities and challenges. Be fearless and engage the opportunities. In today's world almost nothing is forever. So be prepared to take on the next challenge. Success demands intelligence, but substance carries the day and the agenda. Be who you are and be comfortable in your own skin. Follow your own moral compass.

◎ ◎ ◎

Cal HANCOCK, *founder / president, Hancock Gourmet Lobster Co.*

FIRST, CONGRATULATIONS YOU MADE IT! This is a very exciting time, and one to savor. I will just give you a few thoughts about success from my viewpoint. First, let me tell you just a bit about me. I am a woman. I grew up in Maine. I left Maine after high school, but returned after thirty years away. I spent twenty-five years in a career that I studied for in college and grad school, but never felt like it was for me. I was successful in that career if you consider promotions, salary, responsibility, accomplishments. I did well, but I wasn't really passionate about it. Don't get me wrong; I loved the responsibility, the paycheck, the promotions, the accolades, and the work. But I also loved the time away, and didn't always look forward to getting up and going to work each day.

Then I was given a gift. The company I worked for had several layoffs in the late '90s. I kept surviving, but had to tell others they did not. This was not fun. Then I got the news myself. I was somewhat devastated. In the long run, it was the best thing that happened to me. Why? Because from that point onward, I was able to do what I am now passionate about—owning my own company. I started it, I nurtured it, and I love it. I love having something that I call mine. I think about it 24 / 7, and I think that's great. I sometimes don't have enough time or money to do all of the things I want, but I get to prioritize. I smile every day. I have energy every day. I get up every day anxious to get things done. It never seems like work. I don't ever want to retire from doing this.

This doesn't mean you have to own your own company. It just means you should enjoy what you do every day. Just like me, it may take you years to figure out what you really like to do, and that's perfectly fine. You may already know what that is; if so, that's great. You will learn something every day that will help you. Once I started my business, I realized that all the things I had picked up along the way had helped me. Some were ideas that I wanted to use, others were things I wanted to avoid.

Have a great life.

◎ ◎ ◎

Chad STUART, *singer / songwriter*

AS A COLLEGE DROPOUT who somehow stumbled his way to short-lived success in the music biz, I feel ill-qualified to be dispensing advice. I've made every mistake in the book, and somehow I'm still standing. At the risk of seeming redundant, I'm going to have to say that the best asset is tenacity. Life invariably slips you some sucker punches, and the only solution is to "keep on keeping on," as the saying goes. This next bit of advice is not mine; it's from Kid Rock: "Don't hang out with knuckleheads!"

Cheers!

◎ ◎ ◎

Bill RYAN JR., *owner, Oxford Plains Speedway*

MY BUSINESS IS SPORTS, so I always use the same sports analogy: In order to "win" at anything in life, you need to be in "the game." In other words, no one is going to come to your cubicle where you are running statistical analysis for a computer company and tell you that the Red Sox would like you to be their General Manager. No one is going to stop you on the street on your lunch hour and hand you your dream job. In order to get to where you want to be in your career, you need to be in the game. If you want to be in advertising but you are currently working as a barista, you need to attend advertising industry events, read every bit of information you can find on industry trends, and meet people in that world. Sure, some of this will seem pointless. Right up until the day that all of those efforts lead to an interview, which leads to another interview, which leads to a job, which leads to a career. Sitting on the sidelines waiting for someone to see your potential will not work. You need to be in the game.

Charlie ESHBACH, *president, Portland Sea Dogs*

I'M GOING TO OFFER YOU just a little advice. It's something that worked for me, and I think there would be more happy and content people if they took this to heart. When I graduated from college it dawned on me that I would need to get a job. Not just a job, but if I was going to be successful, I'd need to have a career. To me a job was a forty-hour-a-week commitment. A career was a much greater commitment (of time, and self). I quickly decided that if I was going to devote myself to a career, I had better find something I liked to do. Money is important, prestige is nice, but if you don't enjoy what you do, how can you truly be happy?

I've been fortunate; I embarked on a career in baseball administration. At first the money was poor, the prestige an illusion, but the important thing was, when the alarm went off in the morning I was happy to get up and go to work. That's my advice. Find something that when the alarm goes off, you're happy to get up and go to work. As time goes by you'll probably have many of the same joys and concerns we all have: living within your means, getting married, raising children, being a productive and compassionate member of society, lowering your golf score or raising your bowling

"The secret of getting ahead, is getting started."

MARK TWAIN

average—the things that make up your life. You'll do better with all of these if you are happy and content in your chosen line of work.

 Best of luck!

◎ ◎ ◎

Brett WICKARD, *founder / owner, Bull Moose*

THE ADVICE I WOULD GIVE someone who is just graduating from college would be the same advice I was lucky enough to get. As a new graduate, you'll hear a lot about following your dreams, not being afraid of failure, and so on—and that's all good advice—but the truth is, that's only one side of the coin. Those are personal tenets—yet we're primarily social creatures. The person who cares the most about your dreams is you (or your overprotective parents). Other people care more about their own dreams. So what? Well, understanding and deeply appreciating that we're all in this together—and understanding what other folks' incentives are—will allow you to have a more positive impact on everyone around you.

My wake-up call to this idea was given to me by the manager of a local band (whom I'll call "Bill"). I had started a retail business selling music—and as part of that, I thought I would do the community-minded thing of selling all local bands' albums with absolutely no markup at all (i.e. if I bought their record for five bucks, I'd sell it for five bucks). Bill refused my offer of no markup. He wanted me to make something off of selling their record. He felt that if I made no profit, I would have no incentive to truly care whether I sold more of their record or not. While I did care—the reason I was selling local music at cost was because I had a deep admiration and respect for local musicians—Bill's perspective stuck with me. Now, when I negotiate contracts or ink almost any business deal, I keep a close eye on making sure the other party's needs are also being met. While our base instinct is always to fight for ourselves and get the lowest price / most service / whatever—and that works in the short run—I've had better luck—both personally and professionally—by purposefully meeting other people in the middle. You'll find sometimes that you might hold the upper hand while bargaining, and the temptation will be to extract the most favorable terms you can. My advice is to think longer term and forgo a bit of your personal success in the short-run for greater success in the long-run. Overall, you'll be surprised by how many folks who, if you treat them well when you have the upper hand, will turn around and help you out when they have the upper hand. In the long run, everyone ends up better off.

◎ ◎ ◎

Bob LUDWIG, *Grammy Award winner / owner, Gateway Mastering Studios*

I DON'T KNOW if these are words of wisdom, but they work for me:

1. REMEMBER HOW BLESSED YOU ARE. You have probably never gone without three good meals a day and a hot shower when you wanted one. You were born in one of the best spots on the planet, to loving parents who truly nurtured and provided for you. You already possess things the richest king could not buy a short time ago.

2. YOU ARE YOUR WORD. Every word that comes from your mouth. Do not gossip. Mean what you say. Say what you mean, and listen 100 percent to what is being said to you.

When I worked for others in New York, there was a company culture of telling white-lies here and there to smooth things over and not taking responsibility for errors that inevitably occur in business and in life. When I started my own business in Portland, Maine, I told everyone not to lie and it worked. It still works. One can run a business without lying. It is enlivening to be truthful and authentic.

◎ ◎ ◎

Holly NUNAN, *WCLZ radio host / singer*

I'M JUST GOING TO GIVE YOU a rundown of all the things you need to know and understand at any given time. First of all, as clichéd as it sounds, be true to yourself, because no one but you can make you happy. Do not depend on others for your happiness; seek it out and make it your own, because once you become dependent on another individual to make you happy, you are no longer free. And hey, maybe all those Beatles records that you listen to down in your basement bedroom might not be considered cool by your friends, but one day it'll pay off, because you will find like-minded people to spend your time with.

If you want bigger and better things, then go for it. Don't settle just because everyone around you is becoming comfortable and stagnant in his or her own personal situations. Remember, those are their choices, not yours. And never ever, ever give up on music. It is who you are and who you will always be, even if you can't properly play an instrument.

> DON'T CHANGE FOR ANYBODY, BECAUSE YOU'LL FIND THAT ALL OF THOSE PEOPLE WHO GENUINELY LOVE YOU, LOVE YOU BECAUSE YOU ARE YOU AND NO ONE ELSE.

That brings me to your voice: Use it not only to be heard, but also to create beauty and evoke emotion. Use it to get what you want, because as trite as that may sound, you have a power in your voice—not just your rock 'n' roll, foolin' around singing voice—but your speaking voice, your written voice. You will eventually learn how to use all of these skills you think make you so different from everyone else. I know it's hard to think of these personal attributes as skills right now, because they make you feel so singular and alone, and there's no one to really share them with, but keep sharpening them, honing them, because they will get you to where you need to be. You are your most powerful influence, so again, be true to yourself. Don't change for anybody, because you'll find that all of those people who genuinely love you, love you because you are you and no one else.

It's a never-ending journey, but you will find those to share the path with. Be open to life, and always be ready to follow a path you may not have taken before. All right, this has gotten way out of hand with the corny, motivational poster quotes I've embedded throughout, but just keep on keepin' on. George Harrison's words will resonate throughout your life: "Things aren't always going to be this grey, all things must pass, all things must pass away." Eyes ahead, dukes up and heart open: Go get 'em.

◎ ◎ ◎

Chellie PINGREE, *US Representative (Maine)*

THE FIRST THING I want to say to you is this: Always listen to your mother.

Secondly, I think if there is anything I've learned, it's that the place you end up isn't always the place you set out for. When I was raising sheep and growing vegetables as a young woman on North Haven Island forty years ago, I don't think I ever imagined that I would one day be sitting in a room with the president or traveling to a war zone as a member of Congress.

No matter what you set out for or where you end up, one thing I hope you always do is to remain true to your core beliefs and values. Sometimes you might think that what you believe isn't popular, or that others might disagree with you, but I've found that more often than not, people will respect you if you are honest, straightforward, and stick to your guns.

Good luck with the next stage in your life. Oh, and don't forget . . . always listen to your mother!

⊙ ⊙ ⊙

Dan HARRIS, *co-anchor, weekend edition* Good Morning America, *ABC News*

MY CAREER ADVICE IS THIS: Take risks. You're young; you can afford to take a few hits. Set your sights on something that makes you unspeakably psyched, and go for it. You'll have the rest of your life to take humdrum jobs. Now's the time to fantasize about the coolest thing you can imagine being or doing, and then make a good, hard run at it.

Good luck!

⊙ ⊙ ⊙

Christiane NORTHRUP, MD, *physician / best-selling author*

FOLLOW THE PATH OF YOUR HEART—do the things that move you to tears. I went into obstetrics and gynecology because I wept when I first saw a baby born. Nothing in medical school had ever moved me like that. And through the years, I have found that my emotions are my inner guidance system. When I move my feet in the direction of what moves my heart, I do well.

The second thing is this: Your definition of success must include love of some kind. If it doesn't, you need a new definition.

Here's something I know for certain. You chose to be born at this time of great change on the planet. No one alive today has ever experienced the kinds of rapid change we are going through right now. From Facebook to YouTube to Google to electronic books, it's all new, and it's connecting us globally. Your generation is uniquely suited to carry us all into the next era—an era that will see the breakdown of the old social order, the rise of women and the feminine, and true partnership between the feminine and the masculine.

May you soar into your true destiny.

◎ ◎ ◎

Noah TALMATCH, *restaurateur*

THE BEST AND MOST HONEST ADVICE I can give to future generations is to be a failure.

There isn't a successful man or woman throughout history who hasn't failed miserably at something. Without failure, you will never know true success, because those who have never failed, never tried. Only through your failures do you learn the real secrets of success. It may seem dire, sad, and hopeless while you are in the midst of failure, or directly afterward, but you should embrace it with everything you've got. It is your friend, it is your teacher, and it will prepare you for future conquests and great life achievements.

It will cause you to think, to question, and to examine everything that you did. And in doing so, it will make you a much wiser, much more determined, and better-prepared person. One day you will look back and realize that there was in fact a reason for every failure in your life. Those failures will ultimately deliver you to your success.

◎ ◎ ◎

Dahlov IPCAR, *artist / writer*

I WOULD LIKE TO GIVE YOU some "Words of Wisdom" to guide you on your way, but unlike Mother Mary, words of wisdom do not come easy to me.

I feel I have been lucky all my life—lucky in knowing from earliest childhood what I wanted to do when I grew up. I wanted to live on a farm, and that's what I did. And I was lucky because I was born into a family of artists who created beautiful things and made me feel that creating art was just the natural way life should be.

The farm life I lived for almost sixty years was old-fashioned. A nineteenth-century life. We had very little money; it was hard physical work, but it never seemed hard to me because I felt romantic about it. Even with all the farm work, I continued doing my art. I am ninety-six, and I still paint every day.

Winston Churchill once said words to this effect, "For most people their work and their pleasure are separate. But for some people, their work and their pleasure are the same, and they are the lucky ones."

Though I've lived a long life, I'm no Wise Woman. I have no great wisdom to impart. Just do your own thing; don't follow the herd. To hell with fashion. Do the work you love—if you know what that is. You may not become rich, but you will be one of the lucky ones.

◎ ◎ ◎

Anouar MAJID, *author / vice president for global affairs at the University of New England*

ANYTHING THAT IS SAID in this book of wisdom has been pondered for millennia. Nothing will be new—except your being in this world, enriched by knowledge recently acquired in old / new temples of learning. What you got out of your college education is not a skill, but a mind-set. One that will allow you to look at everything differently. Your education has prepared you—I hope—to approach life as a book that needs deciphering. Everything within your grasp contains a story, whether it is the cup you hold in your hand, the laptop you carry in your bag, or the person you spend time with. You are now standing in the middle of a large, borderless canvas, about to paint your journey. You are also in front of an invisible keyboard, typing your experiences in a celestial memory card. Find a good job, make money, and pay the bills. But the quality of your life will depend on the degree of imagination you bring to it. A good, rich, open mind is what you need. Remember that.

◉ ◉ ◉

Angie HELTON, *owner, Northeast Media Associates*

HOW MANY TIMES have you heard or read about the CEO of a successful company starting out in the mail room (or the equivalent)? My mail room was the local McDonald's when I was in high school. I quickly became "The Drive-Thru Queen" because I could take an order with my fancy headset while bagging several Big Macs, fries, and shakes for the previous three orders that were already in line, never forgetting the special sauce, all within 30 seconds. I went from "The Drive-Thru Queen" to "The Multi-Tasking Queen" when I started working at WLBZ-TV Channel 2 in Bangor as an Associate Producer for the news. As an AP, I did everything from editing video tape, to writing scripts, to running the teleprompter, to fetching coffee for the on-air talent.

From Bangor to Portland to New York, I was able to use the skills and instincts I picked up at McDonald's to become an Emmy Award-winning producer for an investigative news team, a job which requires one to research, coordinate, assign, write, and edit several stories at once. And now,

I am in my sixth year as proprietor of a public relations firm, Northeast Media Associates, and have hired my first part-time employee. I owe a lot of my success to some of my first training under the Golden Arches, as well as the Peacock in Bangor.

The lesson I learned, and one I would pass on to young people as they begin their life's work, is to take the best from each experience, no matter how seemingly insignificant; keep your eyes and ears open—be a sponge. Learn from the people around you who can help grow your career and take risks!

◎ ◎ ◎

Bob CROWLEY, *AKA Survivor Bob*

I AM NOW KNOWN as the guy from Maine that won on the television show, *Survivor*. Let me tell you how that happened. I have been extremely lucky and blessed with my careers. I graduated from the University Of Maine-Orono with a forestry degree in 1976. I was unable to find a forestry job after graduation so I starting working for the US Department of Agriculture looking for an infestation of Browntail moth in Casco Bay. I was at the lowest pay scale of all the government workers in America, but I had to pay the rent and buy groceries. It was an interesting job which required me to walk the entire coast of Casco Bay and all its islands. It seemed like an insignificant job at the time but I enjoyed being outside. Two interesting things happened during the time I worked for the USDA.

First, I found an ancient Indian burial site. I reported the location to the state archeologist. The state archeologist forwarded my name to the Smithsonian Institute without my knowledge, which resulted in my becoming the first mate on a Smithsonian research boat, which spent two summers in Labrador and the Northwest Territories.

The second thing that happened was a very bad ocean storm that hit Maine in the winter of 1978. It destroyed many wharfs, homes, floats, and barns along the Maine coast. I was still surveying the coast of Casco Bay at the time. I starting collecting the building materials that were floating ashore and bringing the material out to the island I grew up on as a kid. I built a camp with all that salvaged material. Later, a person that would eventually get a job working for the *Survivor*, saw the camp I made and in February 2008 suggested to the producers that I should be on the show. So, the moral of the story is: Sometimes a job that may seem insignificant at the time can end up making a big difference in your life. I always worked hard, paid attention to my surroundings, was nice to everyone (even when I didn't want to be nice), and remembered that a smile could get me through more doors than a frown!

Work hard, be nice, smile a lot, and don't use credit cards!

◉ ◉ ◉

Judson D. SMITH, *Ed.D., psychologist / Jake's dad*

IN THIS BOOK you have countless people writing to you with words of wisdom and advice. But, regardless of their fame and celebrity, not one of them can say what I can say to you as a father. At this point in your young life, you have accomplished a lot, grown so much, and learned many things—but you're still very young, and you can still use a little fatherly advice.

Remember that the love and generosity of family is something to be cherished and valued. When the chips are down, they are the ones who will help you pick them up. Others may offer to help, but only family will truly come through for you.

As a father, I learned just how much health and wealth are related, so take care of you. You can't take care of anyone else if you don't take care of yourself. Value your well-being, and value your money. Don't be careless with either. Once they are gone, it's hard to get them back again. So follow the old adage and "be healthy, wealthy, and wise."

A gift that many who have achieved great success possess is the ability to be comfortable with folks from all walks of life. Learn to mingle easily with people, lead proudly, and always have the support of others in all your endeavors. Feel what it is like to walk in another's shoes. Empathy is a gift not to be taken lightly. Develop it from within so that it becomes real and not affected, then cherish it and use it wisely.

Stop and think before you simply accept an edict from a person, corporation, or government—or even a sign, like the whites only notice I encountered at a doctor's office in Virginia in the '60s.

Remember that not every instruction is right or healthy or fair. Don't ever accept an unfair rule or regulation without further scrutiny. As Churchill said, "You have enemies? Good. That means you've stood up for something, sometime in your life."

YOU CAN'T TAKE CARE OF ANYONE ELSE IF YOU DON'T TAKE CARE OF YOURSELF.

Fall in love with someone who is intelligent, compassionate, and funny. But falling in love is easy; the secret is staying in love. Be attentive, but not smothering; have passionate interests away from each other so you can bring that excitement back to each other to share; look forward to being together no matter how brief; be generous with respect; talk through every issue; show your love and appreciation; work hard; be financially and emotionally protective. As a media psychologist, I once wrote, "Marriage is not a 50 / 50 proposition. It's each person giving 100 percent." Do that and you will have a long, joyful, loving relationship that will sustain you through all of life's roller-coaster rides.

Finally, when you become a father, be there for your children. Be present always. There should be nothing they can't come to you for, nothing they can't ask you, nothing you won't do for them. Always have their best interests at heart; always keep their confidences; always, always love them.

Brian DEAN CURRAN, *former US Ambassador to Haiti*

RATHER THAN GO ON to graduate school or enter immediately the profession for which you have been trained, consider a two-year break to serve in the United States Peace Corps. Founded by President John Kennedy, the Peace Corps has stood for service to the world's poor for over two generations. But it is much more than that.

If you elect to serve, you will have an extraordinarily broadening experience. You will learn a culture different from your own and experience it daily in a village or town in the Third World. You will learn the reality of globalization and the daily fight for existence faced by the poor. You will help people to surmount health challenges by your example. You will impart knowledge in a specific area (there are many to choose from), and help people to improve their quality of life. You will make lifelong friends, both in the country in which you serve and among your Peace Corps Volunteer colleagues. You will learn another language, which will make it easier for you to learn others later in life. You will travel to countries in the region where you will serve which you may never have dreamed of visiting. You will become self-reliant. You will serve our country and come home able to participate in our national debates on international development and world events. And you will return a more fully developed person yourself.

Take a chance. It will change your life.

John and Karen BALDACCI, *former Governor and First Lady of Maine*

JOHN SAYS "life is like a glass half full, you either see it as half full or half empty, it's your choice." I refined the saying to "you get what you give in life." Both quotes mean you define who you are, you have that power. Be thankful for the many blessings you have been given. In life we have many destinations but it is the journey, the challenges, the mistakes we make, that define our character and who we are. It is this knowledge that gives us meaning to our lives. Listen to the voice inside of you. Trust your gut instincts. Listen to your moral compass. If it doesn't feel right, it most likely isn't. You are just beginning your adult life in an ever-changing world. Be resilient, be flexible, and accept that at times there might not be answers, but more questions and that's okay. We wish you well in your future endeavors and in whatever it is your future holds for you.

"Our greatest weakness lies in giving up.
The most certain way to succeed
is always to try just one more time."

THOMAS A. EDISON

Don CAMPBELL, *singer / songwriter / musician*

I REGRET THAT THERE'S A LITTLE BIT of a "dark irony" in my writing this . . . I had a nephew named Cooper Edward Campbell, who at fifteen years of age was tragically killed by a drunk driver. He would have graduated from Cheverus High School in Portland, Maine, possibly to embark on a journey—maybe similar to yours? Here are a handful of things I would have liked to have shared with Cooper.

It is my sincere wish that you will find some of these useful. I was encouraged early on to follow my bliss. My dad always said, "There are things in life you can do to make tons of money, but doing something you really love can make all the difference in your well-being and happiness." My bliss comes from creating music. I'm a full-time singer / songwriter / musician living in Nashville, Tennessee, during the winter and Cape Elizabeth, Maine, during the summer. My wife Tonya is my bassist, career manager, and best friend. Thus far, my dad's advice has been right on.

- ALWAYS LAUGH, BUT ONLY AT YOUR OWN EXPENSE. Never find laughter from another person's pain.

- TRAVEL EVERYWHERE YOU POSSIBLY CAN AFFORD TO GO; It's an unbelievable world to see!

- ACCEPT THAT LIFE IS KIND OF A ROLLER COASTER, WITH TURNS YOU MIGHT NOT EXPECT. Knowing this just helps.

- HOLD A DOOR FOR PEOPLE AND DON'T WAIT FOR A "THANK YOU." You don't need that.

- TRY TO IMAGINE HOW IT FEELS TO BE DISABLED OR CHALLENGED IN ANY WAY, and help those people whenever possible.

- SIT WITH ELDERLY MEN AND WOMEN WHEN YOU CAN AND BE A SPONGE FOR THEIR KNOWLEDGE AND WISDOM. Their stories and lessons are nothing short of amazing. To read a book is great, but when you can speak with someone who was actually at Pearl Harbor, for example, you get really close to the experience.

- THANK A VETERAN or someone presently serving.

- REMEMBER: Dust never settles.

- ALWAYS TRY TO LISTEN MORE THAN YOU SPEAK. (This has always been a tough one for me, but it has worked when I've employed it.)

- HAVE A CONFIDENT HANDSHAKE AND SMILE WHEN YOU MEET SOMEONE. A smile is the nicest outfit one can wear.

- SLEEP ON BIG DECISIONS, but take risks when you feel confident in your gut.

- ENJOY THE NOBILITY OF PAYING OFF DEBTS, and thank the lender.

- THANK THE PEOPLE WHO'VE INVESTED IN YOU.

- LOOK FOR BEAUTY IN PLACES THAT MAY APPEAR UGLY. You'll be surprised.

- SCUBA-DIVE IN THE BAHAMAS with an adventurous friend!

- REMEMBER THAT EVERY LIVING THING IS HERE FOR A REASON.

- TRY TO BE AT LEAST FIFTEEN MINUTES EARLY—always!

- WRITE BACK TO PEOPLE as soon as you can.

- KEEP YOUR ENVIRONMENT NEAT and always put things away.

- DON'T SWEAT THE SMALL STUFF. If you look closely, most "stuff" is small.

- OWN A TELESCOPE to remind you of what's possible; use it often.

- ALWAYS BE KIND AND THANKFUL TO PEOPLE IN THE SERVICE INDUSTRY— food servers, bathroom attendants, etc. Always tip generously.

- BE GENEROUS TO THOSE YOU BELIEVE IN; be forgiving to those who don't know any better.

- CELEBRATE YOUR EMOTIONS THROUGH PASSION; don't bury your feelings.

- CELEBRATE YOUR EVERY VICTORY, and remember to also celebrate the victories of those you love.

- PAY ATTENTION AROUND MACHINERY, and always remind yourself where you are when you're on a ladder.

- WHEN ASSEMBLING SOMETHING, it's righty-tighty, lefty-loosey.

- RESPECT THE THOUGHTS of the other members on your team.

- THINK INDEPENDENTLY ABOUT ISSUES. Don't just vote a certain way because a party says to do so.

- REMEMBER ROBERT FROST . . . and once in a while, take the road less traveled by.

Finally, just three more things . . .

    1. Always listen to your mother.
    2. Always listen to your mother.
    3. Always listen to your mother.

Be safe, enjoy life, and breathe it all in.

Dora ANNE MILLS, MD, *MPH / vice president for clinical affairs, University of New England.*

SOMETIMES KEY TURNING POINTS in your life happen when you least expect them. You just have to be open to receiving the gifts of those times. For me, one of those unexpected gifts came in the form of some advice given to me in 1992.

I had grown up in Farmington, Maine, then left home for college, medical school, a year abroad in Africa, and five years of residency training and working in Los Angeles (what I refer to as the "other LA"). Early in 1992, after fourteen years of living away from home, I was drawn to return to Maine. I wasn't sure why. I had a terrific job that paid well. I lived in a rent-controlled apartment one block from the beach in lovely Santa Monica. And I enjoyed the friendships of a community of young adults all living near each other.

In order to test the waters, I worked for three weeks in Farmington as a pediatrician that January, figuring that this experience would be a good test of my endurance for Maine winters again, and for practicing in rural Maine. I loved it. I loved working with patients and their families from a community that I knew well. I loved being close to family and hometown friends. And, I loved being part of a small community again.

So, when I returned to LA, I made preparations to move back to Farmington. First, though, I wanted to do some more traveling. After moving my furniture to Maine that spring, I left for several months of hiking in the Himalayan mountain range. Because I had enjoyed volunteering with the Missionaries of Charity several years earlier in Nepal, I signed up to volunteer with them again, but this time for a month in Calcutta. So, after finishing several treks and hikes high up in the mountains, I flew to the muggy delta city of Calcutta.

BE OPEN TO THE **UNEXPECTED GIFTS** THAT COME YOUR WAY, **FIND WHAT** ENERGIZES YOUR PASSION, **AND FOLLOW THAT LIGHT**.

For the next month, I worked in the Kalighat, also known as the Home for the Dying, and in the orphanage run by the Missionaries of Charity nuns. Every day started and ended with the volunteers and nuns attending a prayer service at what they call the "Mother House" (the Missionaries of Charity's headquarters). I was surprised that we got to see Mother Teresa at these services. By this time, she was around eighty, fairly bent over, with very gnarled fingers. She shuffled along without picking her knees up much, but she still sat on the concrete floor of the chapel (in typical Indian style; there are no pews or chairs), and was able to get up without much hesitancy. After the morning prayer service, and before the volunteers left for their various assignments around the city, tea was served in the main gathering area, and this was the time that many would crowd around Mother Teresa to ask her questions or hear what she had to say.

At the end of one's stay, it was customary to meet with her to let her know how your volunteering went, and what you had learned from it. So, on my last day, I went up to her and asked to meet with her. She asked me how my time was. I told her that I had learned a great deal from working alongside the nuns, as they had taught me to see through some of the grotesque results of diseases we witnessed, and to try to shine some love and peace onto each person, and see the love and peace they reflected back.

But, I also told her I was bothered by some guilt. I had witnessed a number of volunteers staying on in Calcutta, some of them selling all of their belongings in Europe or the United States and actually moving to Calcutta in order to live and work among the poorest of the poor. I was feeling guilty, as I did not share the same desire. And, in fact, I was increasingly excited to return to Maine, to move into a home I had bought, to work and live in a community I knew and loved well. I was also returning to an area of relative wealth, and although there were many unmet needs, they didn't compare with those in Calcutta.

She took my hands into her hands, and she replied, "Not everyone is called to work in Calcutta. If where you are going, you will work with love and love your work, that is where you are called to be." Those words struck me like a bolt of light. Of course! That's why I was so excited to be returning home to live and work; it was a place I was drawn to, out of passion for Maine and Maine people.

Little did I know that following this passion would also lead to a career in public health, including directing Maine's public health agency for nearly fifteen years.

So, my advice to you is the same: Be open to the unexpected gifts that come your way, find what energizes your passion, and follow that light. (Now, if you can make enough money along the way to pay for your parents' retirement, that's even better!)

◉ ◉ ◉

Douglas PRESTON, *author*

I CONGRATULATE YOU on entering the adult world, and I would like to share with you a quotation from a man who is far wiser than I am:

> "Affirmation of life is the spiritual act by which man ceases to live unreflectively and begins to devote himself to his life with reverence in order to raise it to its true value. To affirm life is to deepen, to make more inward, and to exalt the will to live." —ALBERT SCHWEITZER

◉ ◉ ◉

Elinor KLIVANS, *cookbook author / food writer*

A ROUND TUIT

This is your ROUND TUIT.
Now that you have it, you can
accomplish anything you want. Not having a
round tuit often keeps people from doing things
they would like to do. You hear them say, "I am going to
study for exams just as soon as I get a round tuit." These
people must search passionately, because when you see them
again they are very sad and say, "Oh, I still haven't gotten
a round tuit." Fortunately, I have been able to locate an
extra round tuit for you.
Now you won't have to spend time looking for one. You can
succeed with what you try to do. Others may talk about how
much they would like to reach their goals, but you now
have a great advantage over them, because
you have gotten a ROUND TUIT.

CONGRATULATIONS!

◎ ◎ ◎

Jerry COLPITTS, *actor*

TWO WORDS COME TO MY MIND: FOCUS and LOVE. Focus, as in relentless personal commitment to excel and achieve. Damn the torpedoes, I've got my sights set, and I believe in myself. Love goes beyond and outside yourself. At the end of the day, even wondrous achievement is meaningless without love in your life. Love is what I hope for you through all your future successes.

◎ ◎ ◎

France SHEA, *director of communications, Girl Scouts of Maine*

IN 1912, Juliette Gordon Low formed the first Girl Scout troop in Savannah, Georgia. It was her absolute conviction that girls needed the opportunity to develop physically, mentally, and spiritually. To get the Movement going, she donated personal property to establish a headquarters, remodeled the house to meet the needs of the organization, and established athletic and recreational fields.

Although the organization was still very small, in 1913 she financed a national headquarters for the Girl Scouts in Washington. Thus far, Juliette, a woman of modest means, had sacrificed most of her personal resources to keep her dream for girls alive. Still strapped for funds in 1914, she sold a strand of rare matched pearls that her husband had given her as a wedding gift. The necklace fetched $8,000—a hefty sum in those days! Juliette said, "The girls need scouting more than I need pearls!" Funds unselfishly gained and wisely spent; those were Juliette Gordon Low's pearls of wisdom.

Here are my pearls of wisdom for you: get a life and be generous! I'm talking about an authentic life and a purpose that is a passion. Don't indulge in a manic pursuit of the next promotion, the bigger paycheck, the larger house—because life isn't about having; it's about giving.

Get a life. Be generous. Pick up your cell phone. Send an e-mail. Kiss your mom. Hug your dad. (Get your own place!) Best of luck to you!

◎ ◎ ◎

Geoffrey HOWE, *Howe & Howe Technologies*

ADVICE TO A COLLEGE GRAD . . .

1. ALWAYS DO WHAT U SAY U R GOING TO DO. Very very important. If u say u r going to be somewhere to a friend or coworker, u better be there!! No excuses!! If on the off chance you feel that u may not be able to meet an appointment, then state it right off, no matter how uncomfortable. When you agree to anything and u fail to meet it, u fail, and failing is a big deal. Doing this very, very important thing will set up dependability and TRUST!! Without that you have nothing. As small as it may seem, never ever blow anything off. If u agree to it, u do it!!

2. do at least one thing per day toward ur goal, no matter how small. Never forget. Once u miss one day, ur goal will be lost. No matter how small, do it, even if it's just a phone call, and one day u will turn around and see u climbed Mt. Everest.

3. never ever bitch about a job!! Just do it, no matter how much it sucks, and do it well. If ur asked to make a PowerPoint, do it; don't bitch, and do it well. Then, if five minutes later u r asked to clean a toilet, do it; don't bitch, and do it well. This will set u up as a REAL asset. This will walk u up the chain of command quicker than any diploma, degree, self-intelligence. No one cares about ur degree 3 months after ur hired. The only thing they care about is what u can do for the company; if u can do everything, then u will very quickly become a manager or CEO. This also sets u up as a very respected employee—by ur bosses, yes, but also ur coworkers. Very very important, because then when ur name comes up behind ur back, the talk will be very positive between coworkers and bosses.

KEEP THE DRUGS AND DRINKING TO A MINIMUM, BECAUSE EVENTUALLY THEY WILL STEAL UR DREAM!! THIS IS FOR CERTAIN!!

4. do not back-stab or get involved with trash talk about others. Do not brag about yourself. Work hard, don't bitch, be modest, and others will talk for u!! This is huge . . . Let others talk for u, and respect is gained without u saying a word.

5. keep the drugs and drinking to a minimum, because eventually they will steal ur dream!! This is for certain!!

6. use others' negative energy for ur positive energy. If they say u can't do it, pour everything into it and kick their ass. (But don't rub it in, because they all will know.)

7. family comes before all else. U can build and become the biggest baddest person ever, but if u don't have a family, u have NOTHING!! Don't ever take ur family for granted, because someday u may be alone and only have memories, and they better be good, because u will die with them. Don't underestimate the family, because many many many poor families have a much better life than a rich jerk.

8. DON'T EVER EVER FORGET WHO U R. Never forget where u came from.

9. ALWAYS GIVE BACK. Do not, do not be greedy. Give to the church, give to the poor, give to others that need more than u. I can't underscore this enough. Do u want to be remembered as a rich Scrooge, or as a man that gave all he had to others with love and charity. GIVE BACK. It will also come back to u. Whether it's God that does it, or karma . . . giving back will come back to u in ways that u will never see or understand.

10. DO NOT BE A PUSHOVER. Be nice but serious. Never ever take back an order. If u give someone directions to do something, never take it back. For example, if u tell someone to clean a toilet, never ever take it back. They may say, "Ahhh, I'm sick," or "Can Joe do it instead?" If u make Joe do it instead, then the person u told to clean the toilet is now the boss of u.

11. SAY A PRAYER EVERY NOW AND THEN. Trust me, it works; we r not alone here, and we will answer for all of our actions when it's all over.

If u do all the above and practice it at a young age, u will be a force of good to be reckoned with.

Eva MURRAY, *author*

AS MY OWN CHILDREN wind up nine consecutive years of dormitory life, here's an observation: It doesn't seem to be the team captains and academic competition winners and skinny rich girls who are remembered; it's the good neighbors.

Teenagers and twenty-somethings are reputed to be notoriously narcissistic. That may be an exaggeration. There are a few college students out there who somehow end up as the "go-to" person in their dorm, or on their team, for problems big and small. These are the young people who respond when somebody needs help. They might have an adjustable wrench in their desk drawer, or a useful work history, or perhaps just a calm demeanor and the tendency not to panic. Others sense in them an innate stability, or a "real world" skill set that can be a huge relief when things go wonky.

I wish the expression real world wasn't part of this conversation. When people refer to life after graduation—whichever graduation is the last one—as life in the "real world," it supports this

"A goal is a dream with a deadline."

NAPOLEON HILL

ridiculous notion that life during school is somehow not real. Everywhere is the real world. Everywhere, people need neighbors—neighbors with skills, or tools, or time to offer a sympathetic ear.

To the peer counselors and "team rookie moms" and campus EMTs and patient souls who let their classmates cry on their shoulders without broadcasting it to the whole world, let me offer a word of gratitude. To everybody who helps move furniture up to the fourth floor, or who sits up all night with a friend whose dog has died, thank you is hardly enough. To those who bake birthday cakes and shovel snow and jump-start cars and help roommates with their first income tax returns, would that there were more of you. To those who teach the new kid how to use the washing machine and who convince the suicidal classmate to accept real help, you may never know how much you have helped. To those who visit teammates in the hospital, drive people to the airport, take class notes for the guy with the broken wrist, and repair bicycles and eyeglasses and lawn mowers, a big thumbs-up. To those who serve as the informal computer-tech help desk, you're a "life-saver." To all those who fix things, explain things, put their muscles to work when work has to be done, make the phone calls, make the cookies, or stay up and listen: You are good neighbors.

The world needs more good neighbors.

◎ ◎ ◎

George J. MITCHELL, *former US Senator (Maine) and former Senate Majority Leader*

FIRST, CONGRATULATIONS!

Second, whatever your chosen field, however detailed your life plans may be, of one thing you can be certain: You will be confronted by challenges and opportunities that you never anticipated or expected. Be open to them. It's good to plan ahead, but not to the extent that it leaves you closed to new ideas and options. Many of the major activities in my life were wholly unplanned and unsolicited.

Third, most human beings have a natural desire to succeed, to achieve status and wealth. It's human nature, and understandable. Given the quality of your education and what you've already accomplished, I have no doubt that you'll be successful, by any standard. But as you achieve wealth, status, and possessions, you'll find there's more to life. Leave some time and energy and resources for other activities. Most people find real fulfillment not in status or possessions, but rather in helping others, in a cause (or causes) that is beyond self-interest. I hope you're fortunate enough to find such a cause in your life.

Patrick DEMPSEY, *actor*

HAVE A DREAM. No Dream is too big. Reach for the stars. With lots of hard work, anything is possible, never give up.

Greg ECONOMOS, *senior vice president, Sony Pictures Entertainment*

MY CAREER PATH has been so varied, it's difficult to actually tell how and why I eventually ended up where I am, but in my mind, the final objective was to have my nine-to-six job (who am I kidding!) be something I enjoyed. While that may have taken a while, I am now at a place where I not only enjoy my job (although it's still work), but I also feel that I contribute in a way that only my varied work and educational experience could allow.

My biggest piece of advice, unless you are on a very clear career path, is to get as much experience in as many different areas as you can. You never know what may "hit" you in the head and turn out to be something that you not only enjoy, but that you'll be successful at in the long run.

Second biggest piece of advice: Network everywhere you can! You never know if the person next to you on a plane, at a restaurant, even on a crowded subway, could be the key to your future success. My first break in entertainment just happened to be answering an ad in *Variety* after trying for years to break in, and just "clicking" with the head of the division. I still keep in touch with my past employers—you never where they may be in the future—and that's how I got my second job in entertainment.

Gretchen LIBBY, *executive in charge of business development and global strategy for Industrial Light & Magic*

1. WITHOUT QUESTION, work hard at whatever you do.

2. BE HONEST AND ACCOUNTABLE. Accept responsibility when appropriate, and be cautious when implicating others.

3. NEVER APOLOGIZE. This was the first piece of advice I ever received. Came from a power player in DC. While I think never is obviously too strong, take from it what you will.

4. DO UNTO OTHERS. Respect others and always say "Thank you." May seem basic, but it's not.

5. TAKE GOOD NOTES. No matter how good your memory is, write everything down.

6. GIVE BACK. Help to mentor up-and-coming talent.

7. RECOGNIZE THAT YOU CAN'T POSSIBLY KNOW EVERYTHING. Experience is not just something that older people talk about. Every new lesson goes into your bag of tricks.

8. BE CONFIDENT BUT HUMBLE. Let your work speak for itself.

9. FOLLOW YOUR INSTINCTS. Set goals for yourself, but be prepared to jump if an unexpected opportunity arises.

10. HAVE FUN! Work can sometimes be hard; always look for the silver lining. What emanates from you will excite and inspire others.

◎ ◎ ◎

Les OTTEN, *entrepreneur*

LEARNING FROM THE MISTAKES of others only works if you endeavor to seek them out.

◎ ◎ ◎

Jesse DERRIS, CEO Derris & Co.

1. FIGURE OUT WHAT YOU LIKE TO DO, and you'll find a way to make money at it. I don't mean this in a touchy-feely way. I want to make money. I want you to make money. I decided not to go to law school because I thought I'd have a miserable life being a litigator. I had an older cousin who was just that, and he told me to find something I love and then figure out how to monetize it. You're going to spend 70+ percent of your life working. Like what you do.

2. SAY YES. A LOT. For the first few years anyway. Being hungry is valuable, and it doesn't last forever. Say yes to meeting people. Say yes to new opportunity. Say yes to helping anyone who asks. Say yes to drinks. Say yes to lunch. Say yes to just about everything. I always help people who ask—I meet with them; I network for them; and everything else. Today's assistant is tomorrow's CEO. Bottom line: make the effort. It's almost always worth it.

3. BE WILLING TO WORK. Key differentiator in our generation. Too many of us were taught by our parents just to enjoy our lives; and for many, that equates to laziness. That's a cop-out. If you're willing to work harder than others, you're going to get ahead. It has always been the case, and never more so than now.

4. BE LUCKY. You can be smart. You can be driven. You can be great at your job. You still need some breaks. I was a spokesman on a presidential campaign at age 24. I was a partner in a very successful business at age 30: now at 33, I own my own company. I love my life. I'm great at my job. But you need to have some breaks. I did, and, hopefully, you will too.

◎ ◎ ◎

Habib DAGHER, MD, professor, civil / structural engineering, University of Maine

I FIND MYSELF very privileged to be doing work that I am very passionate about. I have a mission, not a job. I have a hobby, not a job. I do it because it is the right thing for the students, for Maine, and for the world around me. Find something you are very passionate about, and do it for the greater good of the people around you. I regret to hear people often say, "I am ready to retire from my job so that I can do what I really want to do." It makes me think: "What have you been doing for the past forty years?" Let your job be what you really love to do; then you will never want to stop!

Michael MICHAUD, US Representative (Maine)

FOR TWENTY-NINE YEARS, I worked at Great Northern Paper in East Millinocket. I went to work in the mill like my father and my grandfather before me. There was a time when I was lucky enough to work with my dad. I drove a forklift, and my dad's job was to fix it. I learned really quickly to take care of that machine, or else I'd hear about it at home.

The lesson, I think, is that we are all responsible for our own actions and for taking care of one another. The way we go about doing our jobs or conducting our lives matters to other people—sometimes directly, like with my dad, and sometimes in a more indirect way. We all should be mindful of that and set out to treat each other with respect.

I would add that it's important to be unafraid and to be willing to take risks, whether it's starting your dream business or running for public office, like I did. When I ran for Congress the first time, there were all kinds of people who told me I shouldn't run: I wasn't from the right part of the state; I didn't have the right job, or enough money. Even good friends told me that a millworker could never get elected to Congress. No matter where you come from or what challenges life might throw in your path, you and you alone decide where you want to go and what you want to be.

Hannah HOLMES, author

FOR MANY YEARS I lived by this:

> I would think how words go straight up in a thin line, quick and harmless, and how terribly doing goes along the earth, clinging to it, so that after a while the two lines are too far apart for the same person to straddle from one to the other; and that sin and love and fear are just sounds that people who never sinned nor loved nor feared have for what they never had and cannot have until they forgot the words. Like Cora, who could never even cook.
>
> —WILLIAM FULKNER, *As I Lay Dying*

When I got married a few years ago, I added this:

> It's holding tight, letting go,
> It's flying high and laying low.
> Let your strongest feelings show,
> And your weakness, too.
> It's a little and a lot to ask,
> An endless and a welcome task.
> Love isn't something that we have,
> It's something that we do.
>
> —CLINT BLACK, *"Something That We Do"*

Perhaps it's a peculiar theme for a writer, a spewer of words. But perhaps writers are particularly aware of the silliness of words compared with actual work.

James "HUEY" COLEMAN, *filmmaker*

IT IS QUITE A THING, growing up. I mean, I still feel I am growing up in the sense of learning new things and how to handle new situations I face in life.

Even though this is a big change, a graduation from one stage of life to another, things don't stop or get all set in place or become easy all of sudden. It is because someone like you—and I like to include myself in that category—is always looking for new challenges, new mountains to climb, new oceans to cross. It is the juice that drives the creative spirit. It is what fuels our curiosity. It is what keeps us active and looking forward to the next thing we can try in life. To me, that's what life is about—the next thing.

But wait a minute; first, you need to be in the present. To feel the thrill of living in the moment and the resulting sense of accomplishment. Okay, now we can go on to the next thing.

Hold it again; put on the brakes. What about the past don't we learn from the past? But that again is what drives me to go forward. The desire to improve and raise the level of quality the next time. Each film I make, I feel a step closer to getting it better and better.

Finally, just as people helped you to get where you are, it is now incumbent upon you to pass on hope and wisdom to those that follow your steps. You need to continue that cycle of learning.

So, learning from the past, living in the present, passing on knowledge, and embracing the future. I guess that covers it all.

Good luck. Most of all, keep on doing what you do best.

Bob MARLEY, *comedian*

FOCUS ON THE ART OF THE WORK and not the business. Don't worry about people who say "no." Expect that. Find the "yes" people. And whatever you do, don't forget to have fun!

◎ ◎ ◎

John COLEMAN, *president, The VIA Agency*

WHEN I BEGAN MY CAREER after college, I was thrown into a nine-month training program with twenty-five other new hires who had come from more "prestigious" universities from across the country. I was intimidated at first, I must admit. I didn't want to be left behind, or called out as a fraud. So for every task we were charged with, I began to ask myself a very simple question after completing the work: Did I surprise myself? I found that this simple challenge focused me to use my creativity and determination to discover fresh and different ways of learning and performing.

For example, if we had to give a presentation on a topic we were studying, I would try to present the materials in a way I had never seen done before. If my first attempts were good, but expected or safe, I would go back to the task, always trying to find the guts to take a risk to do things differently—better. I began to find my own voice, my own way of working. Though I was never the smartest person in the room (which you will discover is the norm, not the exception for the vast majority of us), I was often the one standing out because I had found a unique way to attack the work.

As I have gone through life, this simple guiding idea has led me down a wonderful path of constant personal growth. When you do things that surprise yourself, you discover the limitless potential that is in you. Sometimes this is a hard and humbling process. Other times it releases an exhilaration that can barely be withstood. But in the end, what you discover is that you become more and more fearless, open and free from outside dependencies. Which, ultimately, becomes the best way to find the life you were meant to live all along.

◎ ◎ ◎

Jeff KLINE, *Emmy award-winning writer / producer*

YOU'RE GOING TO MAKE MISTAKES. And bad decisions. And publicly embarrass yourself. Because—spoiler alert—you don't know everything. And even if you did, the world would still sometimes conspire against you. So, you might as well live and work aggressively enough to fail. Spectacularly, perhaps. Because the alternative isn't only wholly unrealistic. It's damn boring.

◎ ◎ ◎

Kim L. GRABINA-COMO, *manager, News Partnerships, NBC Universal*

WHEN ASKED TO SHARE some words of wisdom to college graduates, I felt a ping of jealousy. I thought, "how amazing would it be to wipe the slate clean again and start fresh?" With your college diploma in hand you are about to do just that. You will enter a world that is WIDE open to you— one where the possibilities are endless! So now for my words of advice:

- When you choose a career, don't ever give up! REMAIN PERSISTENT & FOCUSED—keeping your goals ahead of you at all times! The road might be long and unpaved—but the journey and how you approach it, is half the fun!

- No matter how bad an experience may be, you never want to burn bridges.

CONTACTS, CONTACTS, CONTACTS! Don't be afraid to use the people you know, or for that matter people you don't know. Someone once told me that you "use people in your life for what they can give you". And as brash as I once thought that was, I now understand it. If someone can help get your resumé to the top of a pile, or help you secure the interview—let them! Ultimately, you still have to get the job yourself!

DON'T TAKE A JOB FOR THE H-LL OF TAKING A JOB! If a job is not right for you, you will know it in your heart & soul. Yes, having a paycheck is nice, but loving what you do is SO much nicer.

There are the simple things like: DON'T BE AFRAID TO TAKE CHANCES & FAIL. ALWAYS STAND UP FOR YOURSELF! I really could go on and on, but the best part of the next step of your life is that it is UNKNOWN!   So I leave you with some words of wisdom from the iconic newsman, Tom Brokaw: "You are educated. Your certification is in your degree. You may think of it as the ticket to the good life. Let me ask you to think of an alternative. Think of it as your ticket to change the world."

◎ ◎ ◎

Bradford KENNEY, *executive director, Ogunquit Playhouse*

EVER SINCE I WAS very young I have been someone who looked forward, and in doing so, wondered, "Where am I headed?" Some would call this gift (or problem, depending on the point of view) as an element of a person who is a visionary or a dreamer.

But when I was in my late teens and early twenties, it also manifested itself in what some would say was a lack of focus. I could not imagine what opportunity was coming that might be right for me. I tried many jobs, and thanks to a great dad who taught my siblings and me the power of a great work ethic, I generally succeeded, but never felt satisfied. Internally, I continued to look forward to something unknown. When my dad saw me going through this, he gave me a book, *What Color is Your Parachute?* He thought it would help me find some of the pieces of crusty bread that would show me the way through the forest of youth. The book is still published today, and I recommend it.

> KEEP YOUR EYES OPEN FOR ALL THAT IS AVAILABLE TO YOU, HAVE A GOOD WORK ETHIC, BELIEVE IN YOURSELF, AND YOU TOO WILL FIND YOUR FOCUS, CLARITY, AND FUTURE.

I soon followed a new course and worked in travel and tourism, working initially in customer service, and eventually in international contract negotiations. And although I was able to travel the world while working, I still yearned for something else, something around the next corner.

Throughout this time, and ever since I was young, I enjoyed theater and art. As a child, I remember acting in melodramas and also sketching by my mother's side in art museums. I continued to act throughout my adolescence and into adulthood. My passion for the arts only grew over the years. When I had risen to a prominent position in the travel industry, I was presented with an opportunity to become a part-time associate producer for a professional nonprofit theater. Even though it meant leaving the job I had, working for a fraction of my salary, and risking everything (a mortgage on an historic home, a luxury foreign car, and all the trappings I had worked for), the thing I had been searching for had finally appeared.

Since then, I have never looked back. Although I do look forward every day now, it is with a clear sense of purpose and vision for the organization that I run and where I am taking it, while enjoying one of the most wonderful careers in the arts I could have hoped for. I have had many parachutes, and am thankful for the incredible opportunities they afforded me, but at the dawn of middle age, I returned to something that was a great love, took a risk, and in my forties, found my clarity and focus.

So, keep your head up, don't worry about having all the answers now (the questions will continue to change anyway), and keep risking new things! Keep your eyes open for all that is available to you, have a good work ethic, believe in yourself, and you too will find your focus, clarity, and future.

◎ ◎ ◎

Josiane GRÉGOIRE, JD, assistant dean, NYU

ONE THING I HAVE LEARNED at mid-life, from my daughter, and also from some of the great students that I have had the pleasure of working with, is to be open to recognizing serendipity as an invaluable gift (or lightbulb moment!) that can take you away from your master plan to where you were perhaps meant to be: a serendipitous meeting can lead to a lifelong friendship or love, or lead to a life-changing opportunity or realization or decision; a serendipitous conversation can inspire or lead you to an entirely new direction, away from your initial check list. My advice is to be open to life's unscripted moments.

◎ ◎ ◎

"Nothing is impossible, the word itself says 'I'm possible'!"

AUDREY HEPBURN

Jim STOTT, *founder and VP, Stonewall Kitchen*

I'M OFTEN ASKED the secret to Stonewall Kitchen's success. How did two guys who majored in child psychology and philosophy, with no business training and no start-up money (literally, "not a pot to piss in"), make the most-awarded specialty food company in the country with customers all around the world? Ignorance was our friend. While it's important to be "planful", it can also be stifling. If Jonathan and I had ever realized all the things that would be involved to get to us to where we are today, we probably would have thought it impossible and never even tried.

LUCK ISN'T WHAT HAPPENS when the Good Witch of the East taps you on the shoulder. Luck is being prepared, aware, and ready to seize an opportunity when it comes along. If you keep yourself attuned to it, you'll be surprised how often luck can happen.

WORK IS WORK. If it were a vacation or a walk in the park, they would have called it that. Work, done well, can make you just as happy.

SURROUND YOURSELF WITH PEOPLE WHO "DRINK THE KOOL-AID™" and possess skill sets that fill in where your abilities are light.

FIGURE OUT THE GOAL, THE TARGET. Fix your sights on it like a laser beam and Do Not Waiver. It is so easy to get distracted and lose your way.

MOST IMPORTANT OF ALL—AND I CAN'T STRESS THIS ENOUGH—DO WHAT MAKES YOUR HEART SING! At the end of the road that's all that will really matter. People who are full of passion are infectious. Customers, clients, and lots of cool people and situations are drawn to happy, passionate, infectious people.

Happy trails . . . Serendipity is waiting for you to find her.

◎ ◎ ◎

Kathy WHITNEY, *former senior public relations representative, L.L. Bean*

BE KIND. Don't be too quick to criticize others or to take offense, and don't take yourself too seriously. When things feel out of control, stop and take a deep breath. When you feel most uncomfortable, it is often when you are growing the most. Everything worth pursuing begins with some degree of discomfort. Don't be afraid to be uncomfortable. Measure your words. You can't regret what you don't say. Be yourself—you are the only person uniquely qualified for the job. Follow your heart and your passions, and mentor others who follow. Be generous and hold onto the things of this world with a loose grip. There is great power in generosity of spirit, of wealth, and of time. Laugh as often as you can, it is good for you and everyone around you. A sense of humor will take you far. And above all, love. Share yourself with abandon, and receive love with the same abandon. You will open a world of possibilities you never knew existed.

◎ ◎ ◎

Linda GREENLAW, *author*

FOR WHAT THEY'RE WORTH, here are a few words of advice for a graduate:

1. OPPORTUNITY is the single most important word in the English language.
2. EDUCATION is never wasted.
3. SUCCESS can't be measured in dollars and cents.
4. MAKE YOUR AVOCATION YOUR VOCATION, and you will be fulfilled.

Only took me fifty years to figure this out. Good luck!

◎ ◎ ◎

Elizabeth PEAVEY, *writer / performing artist*

AS SOMEONE WHO´S been working on a memoir entitled *All the Right Mistakes* for the past ten years, I am usually the last person to give kids advice. In fact, I'm a little shocked to be asked. But, I'm going to go ahead and write this letter. Just remember I'm not necessarily advocating any of these things; your outcomes might differ. With that said, here goes:

1. WORK AT A CRAPPY JOB.

I probably don't need to tell you this one. I imagine you've already been there. But as a writer, I've culled a great deal of material from all the bad jobs I've had over the years, from hatcheck girl to night watchman. People who haven't suffered sufficiently are boring to me. And while working a crappy job doesn't exactly constitute suffering, it usually makes one nicer to waiters.

2. BUT NOT FOR TOO LONG.

Character building is one thing. Soul crushing is another.

3. GET SOME BAD ADVICE.

I recently taught a writing workshop to a group of high school students, and during the Q&A one girl asked what was the best advice I'd ever received. Without thinking, I said it was from the head of my high school English department when I was applying to college. He told me that I had neither the talent nor the discipline to be a writer, and that I should plan to major in something else, like occupational therapy. Grudges can fuel an entire career.

4. GET YOUR HEART BROKEN EARLY, AND GET IT OVER WITH.

Actually, the only thing that can fuel a career better than a grudge is a heartache. The first one is always a lulu, so do it early while there's still plenty of spring in your rebound.

5. WHEN THE TIME COMES, MARRY SOMEONE WITH A REAL JOB AND INSURANCE.

I'm kidding here, but only a little. Yes, the bohemian life is romantic—that is, until you break a bone or need dental work.

6. FAIL.

As Samuel Beckett said: "No matter. Try again. Fail again. Fail better."

7. GO.

When all seems lost, quit your crappy job, lose your rebound fling, load up your car, and get out of Dodge. (See "last person to give kids advice" above.) Bad jobs, broken hearts, trials, failures, rejections, dejections, refusals all look better in a rearview mirror. Just don't forget to fasten your seat belt, eat lots of green vegetables, and call home regularly.

8. DREAM BIG.

The one thing that has always carried me through my crappy jobs, bad boyfriends, rejection slips, wrong turns, and empty checking accounts was the fact that it all felt like it was for a good reason.

9. ALIGN YOURSELF WITH GOOD PEOPLE.

One of the greatest pleasures my writing life has afforded me has been getting to know people I would probably not otherwise meet—that is, unless I was waiting on them.

◎ ◎ ◎

Kirk WOLFINGER, *producer / director, Lone Wolf Documentary Group*

LOVE WHAT YOU DO. Get the kind of satisfaction from your job that you can't distinguish from the rest of the good things in your life. My job is certainly an easy one to love. I don't have a job as much as I have a lifestyle. And the people I know who really seem happy are the ones that love what they do . . . be they teachers or farmers, fisherman or astronauts.

You are lucky to have been born when you were: not too long ago if you veered from your chosen profession or career path, it would have been perceived as a failure . . . now, it's understood that people are allowed to go after the kind of work they want to do, not simply the kind they HAVE to do.

◎ ◎ ◎

Chris BROWN, *head of marketing, Bull Moose*

DO THE RIGHT THING. Why? Because it matters to other people.

Do the right thing in both your personal and professional lives. Doing right has different meanings in different contexts, but it all comes down to being ethical, doing things well, and treating people with kindness. Not only will you feel proud to be a good person, but you will also find yourself surrounded with responsible and conscientious friends and coworkers.

It can be hard to know what the right thing is. Try to figure it out. With practice, you can develop your ability to know what to do. You also will build the habit of doing well. Make a habit of doing the right thing. Doing the wrong thing—being mean, selfish, or lazy—can become a habit as well.

Good and bad habits are easy to form and hard to break. I used to pronounce Mozart incorrectly. I cringed every time I did it in front of my music professors, but I did it for months. Fortunately, I also had the habit of showing up on time and trying my best. I spent two summers as a "sanitation engineer." Both of my bosses were terrible. The first was usually late and / or hungover. My next boss spent most of his time in his office, cheating on his wife with a member of our crew.

DOING THE RIGHT THING ALSO MEANS TRUSTING YOUR INTUITION. SOMETIMES YOU HAVE TO DO WHAT FEELS RIGHT WITHOUT KNOWING IF IT WILL PAY OFF.

I could have been as useless as my bosses were. Instead, I did what I was hired to do and learned a valuable lesson: What I did and how I did it mattered. My bosses didn't care, but the people whose previously trashed floors looked brand-new appreciated the extra effort.

Those jobs stunk, but the next one was really cool. It was the perfect college job for me. I took it seriously, but I did not think it would turn into a career. I wanted to move to New York, so I quit when I graduated. Four years later, my old boss tracked me down. The company had grown a lot since then, and he practically begged me to come back. That was eighteen years ago, and I will be here until I retire.

Doing the right thing also means trusting your intuition. Sometimes you have to do what feels right without knowing if it will pay off. Some of your biggest successes may come from making something fun or interesting and hoping for the best. You might be surprised when some cool, little thing turns into something huge and amazing.

People say that you get back what you put out into the world. I have seen this many times. Whether you are looking for a good romance or a promotion, you will be at the front of the line if you are pleasant and helpful. In the workplace, people favor those who make their jobs easier. Sometimes people will work with you because they have to. If you do a good job, next time they will choose to work with you. Your job will be more rewarding in every way if people want to work with you.

◎ ◎ ◎

Mike CHITWOOD, *former police chief, Portland, Maine*

IN THE GAME OF LIFE, be dedicated and honest, listen and observe, foster a commitment to teamwork, lead with passion, and surround yourself with resourceful, intelligent, and caring people. Success will follow.

◎ ◎ ◎

Michael D. HOWE, *Howe & Howe Technologies*

NEVER FORGET YOU LIVE ONCE. Never forget that life is always a sine wave. Never try to artificially expand or decrease the amplitude of that sine wave . . . Ride it so you can enjoy it, and learn from it—whether you're on the upswing or downswing. Look out the window of your car as you travel down your chosen road of life! Don't get too fixed on trying to control where you're going, because life has a funny way of always putting you somewhere you would have never expected, or prepared for. It's the unexpected that makes life so precious. You'll be truly happy with life if you learn to tilt your prism and use all that you experience to grow, and to not fight what you cannot control. Here are some quotes pulled from my notes that best fit your stage in life:

"Those who are overwhelmed by the finish line fail to see it's the starting line that's most important . . ."

"Happiness is appreciation for what you do have, and not anticipation for what you want . . ."

"We are all users . . . but success is for the few that work to become useful."

Good luck! Work hard and be good to others . . . the rest will fall into place, creating a wonderful life for you that will take you places and give you experiences that you simply cannot imagine now. Who would want it any other way?

◎ ◎ ◎

Lori VOORNAS, *DJ, Q97.9 Morning Show*

MY NAME IS Lori Voornas, and I am a DJ on a morning show in Portland, Maine, and have been for about twenty years now. I guess you could say I'm pretty successful, because sometimes I am recognized at the supermarket.

I have two words for you: high road. There will be times in your life, for the rest of your life, when people are just horrible human beings. They will say hurtful things, they will be lazy, they will be selfish. But if you can always take the high road, and rise above it, you will never regret that decision.

Taking the high road will always lead you to bigger and better things. And sometimes doing it is going to be the hardest choice. Usually the right thing to do is the hard thing; that's why so many people don't choose it.

Bring Kleenex, because sometimes the high road will give you a bloody nose. But in the end, the people you meet on the high road will put your faith back into humanity—and the view is just so much nicer.

To your future. May you, too, be recognized in a supermarket one day.

◎ ◎ ◎

"My grandfather once told me that there were
two kinds of people: those who do the work
and those who take the credit.
He told me to try to be in the first group;
there was much less competition."

INDIRA GANDHI

Ryan PETERS, *AKA, "Spose," rap artist*

TO ANYONE EMBARKING out into the cold world, I offer this advice: Be you. There's so much pressure to imitate those before us. It makes sense. It's how we're raised. As babies, we watch adults around us and imitate their actions to learn how to walk, talk, and interact with others. We are told what to like by the television and whatever's #trending. Boys are told to be tough. Girls are told to be pretty. Wear makeup. Eat here. Be this. At some point you need to stand up and be yourself.

Being you isn't as easy it may sound. In what I do, hip-hop music, there's a tendency to exaggerate or hyperbolize to make yourself sound cooler within songs, social media, and marketing. If I adhered to that prerequisite, I probably would not be able to do this for a living. Sure, I started out imitating and emulating my idols, but sometime after high school, while I was in college at Suffolk University, I decided that my rap persona would be me. And not a superhero, flawless, glossy cartoon of myself, but the actual me. The reason I decided that is because there's only one me. And you're the only you. There's literally no other person on Earth who is the same as you. And that's interesting.

Find what makes you different and cling to it; use it to your advantage. If you do music, especially, this is your weapon. Your uniqueness is all you've got. Hold on to it for dear life and never let it go, because even if you fail, you'll always know you never tried to be someone you weren't.

Other various quick tips: Work on your craft every day, never quit learning, and you have to want it more than anyone else you're in competition with.

◎ ◎ ◎

Mary Ann ESPOSITO, *cookbook author and host of* Ciao Italia *on* PBS.

IF YOU HAVE A DREAM, you will never accept "no" for an answer while pursuing that dream. I know that life is not always fair, but it is what you make of it. I know that to achieve something, you must rely on the faith and friendship of others, for no one is a success unto his or herself. I know that life presents many challenges, but that is what makes us strong. I know that whatever you do in life will affect many who come after you. As you graduate, never forget how you got where you are, and always remember to say "thank you" to those who have guided you this far.

◉ ◉ ◉

Mark BESSIRE, *director,* Portland Museum of Art

GET READY. Life after college is great. You are going to be faced with more opportunities and information to build a career aligned with your life plans than any previous generation. The complexity will be found in how to make the "right" decision for you and your family. Remember, it is good to make decisions, and even decisions that do not manifest the way you first imagined often can lead to your true path. It is better to make a choice and be flexible than to sit on the sideline. A true path is neither linear nor predictable, but it can help you to envision where you would like to be in ten years, to give focus and flexibility to your decisions along the trail.

◉ ◉ ◉

Lou URENECK, *author / journalism professor,* Boston University

THE WORK YOU WILL DO BEST is the work you enjoy the most. Find a project, a job, or a task that engages your interest and your heart. Yes, there will be times when the work is difficult or tedious, but your heart and your commitment will bring you through it. Over time, your life will be richer, and the achievements will naturally follow.

◉ ◉ ◉

Michael LAFAVORE, *founding editor,* Men's Health

WHATEVER YOU WANT TO DO for the rest of your life, do it every day. If you'd like to be a writer, write something daily. If you want to make films, don't let a day pass without picking up your camera. It doesn't matter if anyone else ever sees what you create. It's not about money or recognition; it's about constantly improving.

◉ ◉ ◉

Paul DOIRON, *author*

NOTHING HAS MADE A GREATER DIFFERENCE in my life than perseverance. As a novelist, I subscribe to Ernest Hemingway's dictum: "The hard part about writing a novel is finishing it." But I would add that Hemingway's advice applies to more than just books. Finishing is the key to so many things in life: football games, sales calls, fund-raising campaigns. It is so easy to become discouraged; it is so tempting to give up before the end is in sight. Sometimes quitting seems like prudence. More often, it is an excuse we use to avoid failure. The book that is never finished can never be rejected. Nor, however, can it ever become a success. Seeing a project through to the end is a test of will and a test of character. It is true that we learn a great deal from the process of doing something; the journey can be as important as the destination. But achievement comes from finishing. When you have struggled a long time with hardship and doubt, there is no greater joy than saying to yourself those three wonderful words: "I did it."

◉ ◉ ◉

Pat SIMMONS, *general manager, Cinemagic Westbrook*

Remember to go after what makes you happy.

Keep your sense of humor and do good.

Someone once said that there are times when it's easier to beg for forgiveness than to ask for permission. Know that this is so true!

◉ ◉ ◉

Mike SACKS, *author, humor writer, and magazine editor*

1. TEACH YOURSELF SOMETHING NEW, EACH AND EVERY DAY. No one else will teach you. Or maybe they will. Regardless, don't rely on others. It's really up to you and you alone.

2. READ MORE. Read everything, the good and the bad. You can learn from both.

3. WATCH LESS TV. If you do watch TV, watch what others aren't. There's nothing to be gained from watching the same show that twenty million other people watch. Root around for, say, an old movie on TMC, or a documentary on a subject you know nothing or little about. You could watch a new movie every day for the rest of your life and still not scratch the surface. So many good ones! (And also bad ones, which you can also learn from.)

4. AVOID SODA. It's total garbage, not to mention expensive.

5. EXPERIENCE AS MUCH AS POSSIBLE. Even if this means turning off the TV and taking a walk around the block. Become a flâneur. Don't know what a flâneur is? Look it up.

6. MAKE YOUR OWN COFFEE. It's cheaper.

7. NETWORK WITH AS MANY PEOPLE AS POSSIBLE. Keep in touch with these people. Help each other rise through the ranks. It's not a competition.

8. LIFE IS A LONG RACE. Just because things aren't going well now doesn't mean things won't go well down the road. It's not a sprint.

9. DON'T BE AN IDIOT IN SOCIAL SITUATIONS. How will you know? Do you feel like an idiot? Do you fear that you'll later be looked at as an idiot? Okay, you're an idiot. Stop.

10. NO FACIAL TATTOOS.

11. DON'T GOSSIP. No one gives a shit, and you'll only look like you can't be trusted.

12. DOING NOTHING ALL DAY, EVERY DAY, IS OVERRATED. Yes, it's fun for a month, maybe a few months. After that, it becomes a major, depressing burden.

13. WHEN YOU PARTAKE IN A CREATIVE CAREER, YOU'RE GOING TO BE LEAVING TRACKS. Meaning, you won't be on a traditional career path. In a lot of ways, you're on your own, and you might be looked at as "floundering" or "finding yourself." But to succeed, you have to walk into the wilderness. You won't know what's in there, but that's a good thing. If you did know exactly what to expect, you'd eventually become an accountant or a lawyer. That's not a bad thing, but it's not necessarily a good thing. Either way, this is more exciting.

14. TREAT EVERYONE WITH RESPECT, FROM THE HIGHEST TO THE LOWEST. Do not treat someone poorly because they are an assistant, for example. Who knows where they might be in a few years. Beyond that, it's just the right thing to do.

15. IF YOU HAVE OLDER RELATIVES, talk to them about their lives and experiences.

16. REACH OUT TO AS MANY OF YOUR PERSONAL HEROES AS POSSIBLE. Ask if you can interview them for your blog or website. Some will say yes, others will say no. Keep in touch with those who say yes. When you write to them, however, your e-mails should be very short, and not straining too hard to be funny or entertaining. Just get to the point.

AVOID DRUGS. YOU HEAR THIS ALL THE TIME, BUT JUST AVOID THEM. I NEVER MET A SUCCESSFUL DRUGGIE.

17. WORK HARD, BUT ALSO WORK SMART. Meaning, don't work your ass off with a job that will ultimately get you nowhere. Working ninety-five hours a week at a Baskin-Robbins? Unless you desperately need the money, don't do it. Better to work for free if you're learning and meeting the right people.

18. VOLUNTEER TO WORK WITH SICK OR LESS-FORTUNATE CHILDREN. It will quickly become apparent that your life isn't as bad as you think it is.

19. CONTRARY TO POPULAR OPINION, THE WORD CAN'T should very much be in your vocabulary.

20. NO COLOGNE.

21. IN ADDITION TO A THANK-YOU E-MAIL, YOU SHOULD ALSO WRITE A THANK-YOU LETTER. And send it to the proper address. With proper spelling. And do it within days, not months.

22. AVOID DRUGS. You hear this all the time, but just avoid them. I never met a successful druggie. Or a druggie with an organized apartment and life. You know that friend who owns the huge, homemade bong? The one who sleeps until two ^{pm} every day? You want to be like him? No, you don't. Especially five years down the road . . .

23. TRY TO LOOK AT A SITUATION FROM THE OTHER GENDER'S POINT OF VIEW. Especially when you date.

24. WHEN (AND IF) YOU BREAK UP WITH SOMEONE, do it in person, not through e-mail, texting, etc.

25. FEELING "PUMPED," "PSYCHED," OR "STOKED"? No need to announce it.

26. THERE'S NOTHING WRONG WITH SEEING A THERAPIST. In fact, it's a good thing to talk with someone who has no vested interest in your life or career.

27. IF FINANCIALLY POSSIBLE, spend a year in Rome or Paris.

28. LISTEN TO CLASSICAL. LISTEN TO JAZZ. LISTEN TO OLD BLUES. If you don't like it, fine. But just listen to it every once in a while.

29. BE ADVENTUROUS WHEN IT COMES TO FOOD. Eat anything that doesn't make you sick. Try food from different cultures. Limit your fast-food intake. Avoid prepackaged foods with a ton of chemical ingredients. Again, avoid soda.

30. AVOID SELF-HELP BOOKS (except this one).

31. THERE'S A WHOLE WORLD OUT THERE. There's nothing to be gained from being tethered to e-mail or an iPad or an iPhone all day, every day. Nothing creative will come from such activity. Meet new people. Talk. Listen. Survey your surroundings. Martin Scorsese did not become a success because he checked his e-mail twenty times a day. He became a success because he watched, listened, and, most of all, experienced.

32. JUST BE GOOD. To everyone. To every thing. To yourself. Consistently.

33. IT'S VERY EASY TO CRITICIZE. Anyone can do it. Anyone can tear down. What's more difficult is to create something lasting that will be enjoyed by many. Strive for the latter.

34. A LOT OF PEOPLE, SUCH AS MYSELF, DON'T KNOW WHAT THEY'RE TALKING ABOUT AND ARE OFTEN WRONG. Just because someone gives you advice, that doesn't mean you have to take it. Then again, maybe you should. You'll learn to differentiate between good and bad advice, and soon enough, you'll be giving it to others.

Karen MORGAN, *comedian*

MY BIT OF WISDOM I pass on to you from my father, who left this world much too early but not before he taught me to find humor in all things. He said, "Don't waste your time arguing with crazy people because you will never win—even if you do." He also told me not to "fool around with Mickey Mouse people"—which has nothing to do with sex at Disney World but everything to do with aligning yourself with only the best people in business and in life. There is no substitute for integrity.

> Thoughts become words.
> Words become actions.
> Actions become character.
> Character is everything.

Selma BOTMAN, *special assistant to the chancellor on global education, University of Maine.*

WHEN MY DAUGHTERS LEFT FOR COLLEGE, I told them to join a club or a group of any kind. I wanted them to find people who were passionate about something that they found fascinating. This would, I said, help to shrink the size of a new college or university. Meeting people with common interests in social contexts would help them forge what might become lasting bonds. Not surprisingly, many of the relationships my daughters formed as a result of my advice are still vibrant, and I suspect that some will become lifelong friendships.

You will soon discover that what distinguishes people is not how smart they are or how rich or how attractive. What leads to success in life is hard work. When you look closely at successful people from all walks of life, you inevitably discover that all of them worked hard to achieve their success, while smarter, richer, or more attractive people often fail to live up to their own expectations or to realize their dreams. There is no mystery to success. Work hard if you hope to achieve your goals.

Let me offer you one last piece of advice, possibly the most important: Don't do the obvious. Be adventurous. Take chances. Flirt with the possibility of falling on your face. Those experiences will be the richest, most lasting influences on your life. You will learn so much from them, and they will shape what you become in unexpected, but profound ways.

◉ ◉ ◉

Monica WOOD, *author*

ADVICE? SWEAT THE SMALL STUFF. REALLY. A decent life is composed of small mercies. Send handwritten thank-you notes. Smile at the receptionist. Tell the janitor that the floors look great. Acknowledge the nurse for not making you wait too long, the teacher for teaching you the difference between lie and lay, your best friend for guarding your back. Wave at the flag man when he finally switches the sign from stop to slow. When you start truly noticing people, appreciating the fact that we are all in this together, and that we all have contributions to make—from the guy who cleans the windows of the corner store to the woman who runs OXFAM—every moment gains weight, and life means more.

◉ ◉ ◉

Mark J. WILCOX, *(1931–2013), founder,* The Weekly Sentinel

I HAD THE BENEFIT of a very close family to steer me in the right direction, hoping that I would follow their advice. I knew from the start that I was destined to be a newspaperman, from when I sold papers as a youngster to now, as publisher of my own small community newspaper. I was able to move through the ranks of the large metro dailies to a position of national vice president. I never lost sight of the goals I set for myself.

◉ ◉ ◉

Olympia SNOWE, *former US Senator (Maine)*

IN THE WORDS of the great New Englander, Henry David Thoreau, "Advance confidently in the direction of your dreams." This drive will certainly bode well for the future. In fact, I'm reminded of what I said a few years ago when I was interviewed for a study on leadership, and offered what I believe are central tenets for success and fulfillment:

> Do what you love to do, then figure out what you want to accomplish.
> Don't be afraid to stand alone.
> Believe in what you are doing.
> Follow your passion.

Helen Keller said of true happiness that it was "fidelity to a worthy purpose." And so, as you embark on this new era, remember that the future belongs to those who dare to excel, to dream dreams as vast as America's story itself. With talent, hard work, and determination, the sky is, as they say, the limit.

◎ ◎ ◎

Karen CARBERRY WARHOLA, *director, Maine Film Office*

WHEN I WAS GROWING UP, I didn't plan to work for a major Hollywood studio, nor did I ever dream that I would one day sit in a movie theater and watch my name roll by in the credits, nor fly around the country auditioning singers for a television series, nor work on a show that Brittany Spears would perform on. All this and much more eventually happened to me because I made positive choices along the way that helped to open doors.

Those choices stemmed from the single conviction that the only limitations to my continued growth and development as a person were the limitations that I placed upon myself. As that conviction deepened, so did my determination to seize every opportunity that life presented.

Likewise, before you stand many choices, and the criteria you use to make decisions are the fundamental determinants of whether the choices you make will move you forward and promote your development and growth, or hold you back and stymie you. You will not be the same person in five years—or ten years —that you are today. Where you are in life, and what sort of opportunities you will discover, hang largely on the decisions you make today. The process of shaping the person you want to become does not start tomorrow—it starts now, at this moment, as you decide where you want to go from here.

 The best single piece of advice that I can give you is: now is the time to get out of your "comfort zone." The more often you step outside of your comfort zone, the more often your world will expand and your self-confidence will grow. As your life—and circle of comfort—gets larger, you'll be able to see the big picture more clearly and be more capable of shaping it. Along the way, embrace any experiences that can help expand the world you live in. The knowledge and life experience that makes you unique, will make your personal life richer, and will help make you a more interesting and valuable asset to future employers or business partners. Starting today, decide what would really make you happy in life and go for it. Along the way, embrace any experiences that can help the world you live in get bigger and you'll be better prepared to make the right decisions for you.

Pete KILPATRICK, *singer / songwriter*

LET YOUR PASSION for the things you love be ever present in the back of your mind. Never forget why you started doing these things in the first place.

Stay humble, yet confident. In the words of Henry David Thoreau, "Success usually comes to those who are too busy to be looking for it."

Rich BROOKS, *president, flyte.biz*

NINE THINGS I've learned from being an "adult":

1. IF YOU'RE NOT MAKING MISTAKES, you're not trying hard enough.

2. CONFIDENCE AND PERSISTENCE will get you "there" 99 percent of the time.

3. EVERY JOB / CAREER / RELATIONSHIP REQUIRES YOU TO "PUT IN YOUR TIME." However, if the job / career / relationship isn't ultimately leading to your happiness, cut your losses and walk away.

4. WHEN TRYING TO IMPRESS MEMBERS OF THE OPPOSITE SEX, ask them questions about themselves and let them answer them. Don't interrupt, but stay engaged. They'll see you as the ultimate conversationalist.

5. BUILD YOUR NETWORK. Build it on Twitter, Facebook, LinkedIn, and whatever comes next. With a big-enough network, you can accomplish whatever you dream.

6. MEET WITH A FINANCIAL ADVISOR . . . NOW. The earlier you start saving and investing money, the more protected you'll be down the line. I can't stress this enough: It will greatly reduce one of the biggest sources of stress in your life.

7. TRAVEL. The world is an interesting place filled with interesting people. People who never leave the United States tend to be myopic and uninteresting.

8. TRUST YOUR GUT. Going with your gut and being wrong is only, like, a million times better than going against your gut and being wrong.

9. DO OR DO NOT . . . there is no try.

"Often when you think you're at the end of something, you're at the beginning of something else."

FRED ROGERS

Jeanne PAQUETTE, *commissioner, Maine Department of Labor*

MY ADVICE TO YOU is to remember this: It's not the amount of knowledge you have, it's how you synthesize and apply it. Be resourceful and you'll succeed.

◎ ◎ ◎

Rob DRAPER, *ACS, director of photography*

IT WAS THE WINTER OF 1979. I sat in the lunchroom of a small regional TV station in Wagga Wagga, Australia, reading a magazine extolling the virtues of a new concept in education: one-week "workshops" at The International Film & Television Workshops in Rockport, Maine (wherever that was). Four years into my career, I wanted to know where I stood in terms of the global scheme of things, so in 1980 I packed my light meter and headed off to become the first Aussie to attend these one-week workshops. Little did I know what was in store: a week of interaction with like-minded souls from all over the world. That was amazing in itself, but it was one phrase that changed my path and process forever.

The workshop was being led by legendary Hollywood director of photography Frank Stanley. I was on stage for my turn at a lighting setup, having trouble deciding what I should do. My repertoire was short TV magazine segments, music videos (although I did not know what they were about to become), TV news, and ultra-low-budget regional TV commercials. Frank suggested a simple shot of a man standing under a lamppost, lighting a cigarette, with the flare of the match illuminating the man's face. In those days this was not easy. Slow film stocks and course grain on medium-speed stocks meant everything had to be done with artificial lighting, so I set about lighting the scene.

After forty-five minutes Frank wandered by and asked what I was doing. "Trying to get the match light to work" was my reply. "Doesn't a match work by itself?" Frank asked. "Well, yes, but I don't think there is enough light from a match to register on the film we're using." Frank gave me a questioning look and asked how I knew that, to which I responded, I was guessing. "Well, why not guess that it will register?" came Frank's immediate reply. I was stumped. Good point, but I was still convinced it would not work. I had no reply. "How would you do it?" I asked. The answer was what you might expect: "I'm not doing it; you are."

With that, Frank turned to walk away, took a few steps, then turned back to me. "Rob, you have to do this shot however you think is best, but I will tell you one thing: If you don't take a risk every time you push the button, you are mediocre." If you don't take a risk every time you push the button, you are mediocre.

That simple phrase stopped me in my tracks. I had been hit by a bolt of lightning. I was in control; it was my vision, and I had to push the boundaries. Take a chance. I decided to go for it, pushing the limits like never before. It was so dark, I couldn't even see the guy in the viewfinder. We had to wait three days for the film to come back from NYC. Yeah, that was before digital immediacy, when you had time to agonize over what you had done. Sitting in the darkened theater with forty other cinematographers . . . and Frank. I was a bundle of nerves. Up came the shot. Probably the riskiest shot of anything attempted during the week. It was brilliant. I shocked myself. Wow . . . I actually did that.

> ## THE MOMENT IS WHERE WE NEED TO LIVE IN ORDER TO BE CREATIVE AND TO BE THE BEST.

More than anything in my thirty-plus years in film, those few simple words have been my guiding light. But there was one more element I was yet to discover—an element that made risk-taking fun and easy. During lighting workshops I have taught around the world, I have used many examples of recognizing this element, but one close to home really struck a chord.

I was at a semifinal basketball game; my son's team was down by three points, with eight seconds on the clock in the fourth quarter. They were playing for a berth in the state finals. They had possession. Whistle blew, ball in, one pass, another pass and another, the clock was running down, 3, 2, 1, and a player three-quarters of the way down the court, on the run, lobbed a two-handed shot at the net. The net was almost in the next state. The buzzer sounded and the ball sailed through the air. Spectators were on their feet. Almost slow-motion. The ball did not even hit the backboard; straight into the net, didn't even touch the rim, from three-quarters of the way down the court. Overtime, and they won the game.

What a shot! What a fluke! Couldn't do that again in a million years! The basket was put down to a "lucky shot" . . . chance. But was it?

For a moment in time that player was in the zone. He was playing intuitively, not thinking about anything other than knowing where that ball needed to be. All the math needed were taken care of—nervous impulses, muscle contraction, trajectory, targeting, backspin— calculated in an instant, with no conscious effort. A valuable educational lesson lost to cries of lucky shot.

The moment is where we need to live in order to be creative and to be the best. The moment is fleeting, often simply dismissed as chance, but the people who rise to the top are those who recognize that moment, embrace it, and stretch it to become more than just a fleeting moment in time, forgotten and passed over. Risk-taking leads to discovery. Recognizing and living in the zone allows us to take risks that are always calculated, based on our accumulated experience, allowing us to strive not for perfection, but to attain the maximum from our potential.

You are starting your journey. Take risks, find the zone, embrace it, and live in it. Best wishes for a long and challenging adventure.

◎ ◎ ◎

Robert SHETTERLY, *artist*

IT'S A DAUNTING TIME to be young with one's eyes wide open. I see many students from all age groups who feel grim about the future—their future. I can't refute that grimness. However, because I feel that way, I often recite these lines from Christopher Fry's poem, "A Sleep of Prisoners":

> Thank God our time is now when wrong
> Comes up to face us everywhere,
> Never to leave us till we take
> The longest stride of soul we ever took.

It's a great and noble challenge, not to expect to be a savior. But I think the longest stride now is to embrace cooperation and community. To reject competition. To find ways to build strong, sustainable community.

Probably the greatest crisis of our time, the greatest failure, is the failure of governments to care for people, to be strong enough to reject the power of corporate profit and influence, and to begin to model our economy on the economy of nature, a non-growth, nonprofit, sustainable economy. It's the only hope.

We all must rise to the requirements of our time even when it is not the challenge we would like to confront. James Baldwin said, "People who shut their eyes to reality simply invite their own destruction." Our task is not to shy from that reality. And where we are now is both a real and a mythic moment in human history. It's mythic in the sense that it's the kind of situation we loved experiencing vicariously in *The Lord of the Rings* or the Darth Vader stories. Now it's upon us, and it's harder than we could have imagined.

Grim, yes. But the only way through is in joy and love, determination and courage. The same values we have always admired but never needed so much. One for all and all for one.

◎ ◎ ◎

Rich PATTENAUDE, *president, Ashford University*

WHATEVER YOUR JOB, assignment, or responsibilities, do your work the best you can. In the end, hard work and good work are recognized and rewarded. Good luck to you as you begin the exciting adventure of living and working in today's complex and fast-changing world. Oh yes; don't forget it is okay to have a little fun.

◎ ◎ ◎

Rushworth KIDDER, *(1944–2012) Ethicist*
(previously published © 2001 by the Institute for Global Ethics)

ON SEPTEMBER 11, the terrorist attacks at the World Trade Center permanently altered the New York City skyline. Less noticeably, but perhaps more powerfully, they changed something else: the moral thoughtscape of America.

The intense public cruelty of that day has driven us to the windows of the soul—to new depths of introspection, moral searching, and spiritual questioning. All across this otherwise pragmatic and down-to-earth nation, the air is suddenly filled with oddly metaphysical questions: Who are we?

Why are we here? How do we understand our purpose? What can I do?

That last question concerns the individual's role in the face of evil. That's a profoundly moral question, and for most people, the answer is, "I ought to get involved, lend a hand, help out in some way." But there's a nagging doubt: Can my involvement really change the world? Even if I, and all my friends and all their friends, banded together to help, could we make an impact? Compared to the seven billion people in the world today, we're but a rounding error. Can we really make a difference?

Yes. Let me explain with a kind of parable.

Some years ago, I interviewed a number of people here and overseas for a newspaper series on global education. Among the interviewees were several American men in their thirties. Each had grown up in a terrible ghetto environment. And each, in some way, had "made it" and was successful.

Why, I asked them, had they succeeded? Why had they not been gunned down at age eighteen in a neighborhood alley as, statistically, they might well have been? Each, using different specifics and a different name, told me the same story: It was old Mrs. Smith in the fourth grade who really turned them around.

"But wait," I asked them. "You've just told me about your schooling, where you had dozens of awful teachers. You've just told me about your large and dysfunctional family, where hardly anyone seemed to care. You've just told me about your scores of friends—many now in jail, others now dead—who set all the wrong examples. And now you're telling me that, in the face of that relentless downdrag of depravity, Mrs. Smith alone lifted you up?"

"Yes," each said, "that's what I'm telling you."

In itself, that fact doesn't surprise us. We all know, intuitively, the enormous power of a single right example. The question is, Why should it be so? Why is it not equally true that a child raised in caring, attentive surroundings can meet one bad teacher and be plunged into a life of crime and vice? Somehow that's far less observable.

To understand why, perform the following experiment. Find a closet that's been closed up for years. It's been shut so tight that no light can get in. If there's any place darkness could grow thick and rich and ugly, this is it.

Now, light a candle. Turn off the lights in the room outside the closet. Open the closet door, and watch closely. Does this appalling darkness gush forth with such virulence that it extinguishes the candle and plunges you into utter blackness? No. In the entire history of the world, that has never once happened. Always, unfailingly, the candlelight illumines the closet and dispels the darkness.

That, too, is observable. But why should it be so? Because light is not the opposite of darkness. It's the absence of darkness.

If light were the opposite, we'd be playing a zero-sum game with the forces of anti-light—where, about half the time, darkness would win. Maybe, if we pulled together a thousand candles, we could just barely defeat such a grisly accumulation of blackness—but only for a while, until the closet forces regrouped and came back to defeat the candle.

LIGHT IS **NOT THE OPPOSITE OF DARKNESS.** IT'S THE ABSENCE OF DARKNESS.

Put that way, it sounds silly. Yet notice how our metaphors work to persuade us that darkness and light are equal but opposite powers. We're so used to thinking in terms of opposites—positive and negative charges in electricity, north and south poles in magnetism, up and down, left and right, yin and yang—that we let our metaphors overwhelm us. "Oh, yes," we assert, without examining our premises, "the world is made up of opposites. Light and dark—they're opposites, too. After all, night and day appear to be evenly balanced—in the course of a year, there's about as much of one as of the other. So darkness must be the opposite of light."

That mistake might be relatively harmless were it not for one final logical misstep, where we seize on light and dark as our principal metaphor for good and evil. Result? We think of ourselves as locked in battle with powers of evil that are balanced on a knife edge against the forces of good. What will it take, we ask, to defeat such a terrible force? Surely all the goodness in the world, if we could scrape it together, would barely be enough to overcome this equal and opposite power.

But what if—just what if—we've missed the real message of the metaphor? What if evil is less the opposite than the absence of good? Doesn't that explain how old Mrs. Smith could single-handedly overcome the inertia and emptiness of our young friends' ghetto upbringings? Wouldn't it seem odd, in fact, if evil ever seemed to prevail in final combat with good?

Don't get me wrong. I don't mean to minimize the complexity and perversity of the world's evil. I don't for a moment imagine that the forces of depravity will evaporate just because we shift metaphorical gears—or that, in our current situation, terrorism will instantly disappear because we analyze it in a different way. But I'm equally sure that, until we think clearly about evil, we will never master it successfully. Such clarity begins with the understanding that, however massive the assertions of evil, they bear witness only to an absence, not to an opposite.

And that helps explain something else: That just as a single candle can destroy a whole closet-full of darkness, so a single life, lived in the light of goodness, can make an enormous difference in overcoming the reverberating void that calls itself terror and blackness. If that's the case, is it any wonder that any one of us, accurately assessing the moral nature of reality and banding together with a few others in unity of action, really can change the world?

Rob CALDWELL, *anchor, WCSH6*

NO ADVICE. Just a few quotations I like:

> "Good judgment is the result of experience. Experience is what you get from bad judgment."
> "A person who doesn't read good books is no better off than the one who can't read them."
> "No one on his deathbed ever said, "Gee, I wish I'd spent more time at work."

Shannon MOSS HAGERTY, *television journalist*

THIS IS TRULY AN INCREDIBLY EXCITING TIME of your life. You are about to embark on an amazing journey . . . your bright future, with you at the helm. If I can impart any advice it would be to, sometimes, take the roads less traveled. The views can be quite breathtaking. Remember that the greatest risk is not taking one. And perhaps the most important is to live: live your life, travel the world, dare to dream and do something about it, work hard, and love and laugh the most.

Tess GERRITSEN, *author / retired physician*

BE AN INFORMATION PACK RAT. When you learn something new and interesting, file it away either mentally or in an actual file folder of "cool things." Keep on amassing these disparate bits of info—offbeat news stories, odd facts, items that just strike you as quirky. Because one of these days, you may find a use for one or more of these stray bits of information. Sometimes what looks like genius is just the ability to connect two seemingly unrelated facts and noticing a pattern. Or realizing that if you combine those seemingly unrelated bits of information, you come up with an astonishing new concept.

Tim FERRELL, *comedy writer / director*

1. Wear comfortable shoes
2. Brush after every meal.
3. Stay hydrated.

I've been asked to share some insight and experience I have gained on my road to success for young people who are just starting out. First, we are both the beneficiaries of a hidden advantage: a supportive, loving family. I know for a fact that what your parents have passed down to you will always allow you to learn and work hard and make sense of the world in ways others cannot. To this day I still go to my dear mom for advice.

Road to success?

Well, at times it's hard to even find the on-ramp to that road. My approach has always been to make my own road. It takes a lot of heavy equipment and labor, but it's my road, and I can drive as slow or as fast as I want. Am I successful? That will remain a mystery for others to determine at a later date. Am I enjoying the ride?

Yes.

After much reflection and a fear of clichés, I have just one pearl that has served me well: Who you spend your time with and how you spend your time is what determines what you will become.

So, put on those shoes, pack your toothbrush, and take a swig.

◎ ◎ ◎

Tony V, *actor / comedian*

GOOD LUCK WITH WHATEVER YOU ARE IN FOR. It's gonna be a hoot! No matter how hard or weird things will feel to you, remember to laugh at everything and everyone, including yourself! What makes you think you're better than everyone else? I'm going to pass along some advice as you wander into the labyrinth of adult existence:

1. AS YOU WALK THROUGH LIFE, occasionally look ahead but always look down; there are a lot of dogs in the world.

2. ALWAYS CHOOSE DOOR #1; it's as good as any.

3. IF ANYONE ASKS, you didn't see anything!

4. FAILING IS NO SIN. Not trying is.

5. IF THE CROWD GOES RIGHT, go left or stay where you are; they will eventually end up back with you!

6. THERE IS SUCH A THING AS A "FREE LUNCH"; you just won't like it!

7. SEX IS NO SUBSTITUTE FOR LOVE, but it will do in a pinch.

8. NEVER GO INTO A BANK THAT HAS AN ARMORED CAR in front of it.

9. THE SHORTEST DISTANCE BETWEEN TWO POINTS IS A STRAIGHT LINE. You will see more if you go the long way!

10. DON'T LISTEN TO ANYONE BUT YOURSELF!

◎ ◎ ◎

 Tim SAMPLE, *Maine humorist*

LIFE LESSONS LEARNED ALONG THE WAY: First of all, let me congratulate you on completing a marvelous college career, and extend my best wishes as you embark upon the next phase of your life. I've been asked to pass along some "words of wisdom" based on my own life experience. I'm more than happy to oblige, since it is my belief that in real life, "Experience is the best teacher." Here is just one memorable example of a personal, life-changing experience which I hope you will find helpful and instructive. I sure did!

In 1976 I was twenty-five years old and working very hard to establish myself in the entertainment business. I got a big break when I was offered a gig as opening act for Noel Paul Stookey, "Paul" of Peter, Paul and Mary. The first show went so well that I was hired to do several more, and over the next two years we became good friends. In 1978 I moved to Blue Hill and began working full-time at Noel's company, Neworld Media.

We continued to perform together, and Noel even produced a five-song music album for me. I was convinced that it was just a matter of time (weeks? days?) before I became a big star in the music business! Around that same time Noel was also producing another young singer / songwriter named David Mallett, and in the summer of 1979, Noel, David, and I were scheduled to perform a big series of concerts with several other singer / songwriters. During a break in rehearsals the day before the first show, Noel took me aside and told me that he thought there were too many singer / songwriters on the bill, and that since I had a real talent for making people laugh, I should leave my guitar backstage and emcee the show, doing a series of five-minute comedy bits in between the other acts.

This was a watershed moment. Should I change my act or insist on doing my music? I decided that since Noel was the only person I knew with several gold- and platinum-selling albums, Grammy Awards, etc., perhaps he knew more about show business than I did. It was the right choice. I was very successful that night, and went on to do more comedy bits for the rest of the tour. About a year later Noel produced my first album of Maine humor, and the rest, as they say, is history.

The irony, of course, is that my success as a Maine humorist has given me access to a much larger audience than I would likely have ever had as a singer / songwriter. Although I've continued to perform a song or two in my shows and albums over the years, I've reached millions of people I'd never have reached if I had made a different choice way back in 1979!

◉ ◉ ◉

Jeff INGLIS, *former editor,* the Portland Pheonix

ADVICE TO A YOUNG GRADUATE:

- SPEND AS MUCH TIME AS YOU CAN IN OTHER COUNTRIES. You will learn more about yourself, the world, the United States, other cultures, and humanity in general—and far more quickly—than if you stay at home.

- YOUR HEART WANTS WHAT IT WANTS—in love, in work, in private life, in everything. Listen to your heart, and nourish it, and it will lead you where you most need to go, whether you know where that is or not.

- SPEAK TRUTH. Not just to those in power, but to friends, to acquaintances, strangers, family members. Especially to lovers. Professionally, do your research, bolster your arguments, and stick to them. Personally, search your feelings, find your solid ground, and stand on it respectfully.

- NEVER BE AFRAID TO CHANGE YOUR MIND. And seek out people who disagree with you—engaging with them will sharpen your insights and may, ultimately, illuminate for you a world previously unseen.

- YOU CAN ALWAYS DO MORE, AND FOR LESS MONEY. And the thing you do for next-to-nothing will be the most valuable, most rewarding of all.

- STOP, LOOK, AND LISTEN. This does help at crosswalks, particularly in the United Kingdom and other left-side-drive countries. But take in yourself, your senses, your thoughts, your emotions, the experiences of those around you, your physical and natural surroundings. Feel them in your body, sense them in your soul.

"Be kind, for everyone you meet is fighting a hard battle."
Plato

- HESSE'S SIDDHARTHA HAS A GREAT MANTRA FOR JOURNEYS: "I can think, I can wait, I can fast." (I add one corollary: "I can hold it.") But that mantra is primarily useful for physical transit. When questions of the heart and soul are at play, the only relevant fact is whether your heart and soul are starving. If they are, do everything—anything—it takes to feed them, without over-thinking, without delay, and without holding back.

- INVERT COMMON AXIOMS. For example, there's the whole cliché about sucking the marrow out of life, but it's much more important—and vastly more rewarding—to stop asking what you can get from the world around you, and to start asking what you can give. Spit the marrow into someone else's life—be part of the marrow of someone else's life. You'll learn and grow every time.

- WHEN YOU CEASE TO LEARN, YOU CEASE TO LIVE. Notice if this starts to happen, and reverse it.

◎ ◎ ◎

Joe CUPO, *chief meteorologist, WCSH6*

SEVERAL YEARS AGO I was asked to be the commencement speaker at a high school graduation ceremony. My message to the students was to encourage them to take responsibility for themselves and not wait around for someone or some entity to take care of them. Since I made that speech the number of people on food stamps and other government subsidies has skyrocketed to the point where almost half the population is currently receiving some form of government assistance. I think this is a recipe for disaster and if this country is going to prosper in the coming decades it needs to be changed. All college graduates should be made aware of this dilemma. In my opinion, the best advice came from President Kennedy in his inaugural address. "Ask not what your country can do for you—ask what you can do for your country." That would be my message.

◎ ◎ ◎

David TURIN, *restaurateur*

WHILE YOU HAVE PASSED many milestones in your life, this is a very different one than those you previously passed. You have indeed arrived at a very different place. You have worked hard and stuck with things when they were not easy, and now you have arrived at a place where all of your strength, courage, conviction, vision, passion, decency, moral integrity, honesty, loyalty and brains have gotten you to where you wanted to be. You have an education.

So now that you are here, it's time to show the world what you can do—to unleash all of that tremendous potential, to find your passions, and to follow them wherever they take you. It's time to put all of that practice into action: to leave your mark on the world, to begin building a legacy of something great that you and everyone who knows you will be proud of. Of those with much, much is expected. You have much. You are much. Go forward and know that the world has no specific expectations of you except these:

> BE A GOOD CITIZEN to your family, your friends, and your colleagues.
> DO YOUR BEST, do it with passion, do it with honesty and integrity.
> ENJOY THE PROCESS of doing it.

It may have been Mark Twain who said this (and I loosely quote),

> " Your life is what happens to you while you're on your way somewhere else."

So I say . . . Moments lived now, strung together end-to-end make up a life. Remember to live each one of those moments, because once they pass, they are gone forever.

Jonathan EDWARDS, *singer / songwriter*

THESE ARE INCREDIBLY tumultuous times during which we decided to push you off the edge of the nest and anxiously watch as your wings unfold with unproven strength well before you hit the ground. We sat on your fertilized egg for nine months and fed you food from our mouths for another month or so and there you go . . . flying . . . feeling the greater air pressure on the feathers beneath your wings and taking to the sky. You'll be back, though, when you get hungry, to find out just which bushes offer those seeds you like so much and under what tree those delicious worms can be found and when you need to the answer to, "how do I fly south again?" To advise a fledgling is a matter of generalities and specifics; an exercise in restraint and circumspection. I have learned the only real way there is to learn is by doing. There is safety, security, and strength in the numbers in your flock. Learn to fly among them. Be available to guide them, be open to being guided. Your own wings will gain skill and energy everyday, but listen intently to the voices of the others. Make sure you can identify their sound through the dark of the night or the gales of the storm. The other birds and your relationships with them are the are the key to your success. Avail yourself of the collective consciousness, the group wisdom, the friendships you engender. Recognize the birds that really speak to YOU and fly with them. These are YOUR wings . . . be careful with them, respect them; they will be your mode of living. Nurture and learn from the other birds of your species, the members of your flock; they will be the mode through which you'll thrive.

Susan M. COLLINS, *US Senator (Maine)*

THOSE OF US WHO ARE, are fortunate to be from Maine, where we learned the values of hard work, community, cooperation, and fair play. You will forever have those values as part of you, and they will help you to succeed in the next chapter of your life. In college, you learned not only from books and lectures, but also from your interaction with your broader environment. And you have learned, I hope, that knowledge must be translated into action. Sitting on the sidelines cannot be an option. Your community and country need your active involvement. I challenge you to put the critical thinking skills you have developed to work on the complex national and global issues that we must confront. We are counting on you!

Acknowledgments

IN THE SAME SPIRIT that inspired this book—that no one achieves success alone—I can attest that no one puts together a book like this alone. Thus, I would like to express my deep appreciation to all those who responded to an e-mail from me titled "Favor"—some dear friends, some mere acquaintances—all of whom said "yes," which is of course the first step to any success. I am grateful to each of you for so generously sharing your stories and wisdom with Jake, and every young person just starting out.

I also want to thank Paul Doiron for believing in this project not once, but twice, and Dean Lunt, for believing Paul Doiron.

I am grateful to Fred Nutter, who twenty-four years ago taught me the value of a good editor, and to Genevieve Morgan, for being one.

When I was eight and she was eighty, Martha Hawkes Hill taught me to love words. We would spend endless afternoons together playing Scrabble and doing crossword puzzles. She never tired of showing me how I could make a better word.

I am thankful to all of my colleagues who proved that the real secret to success is to surround yourself with people who are smarter and more talented than you are.

Finally, this book is at its heart about friends and family, and without my family's love and encouragement, it would not exist. So thank you: to my dad, whose sense of humor, unconditional love, and generous spirit are ever present. He showed me how to be Jake's mom. To my own mother, whose harrowing story of escape from behind the Iron Curtain is still one of the best stories ever told, and the inspiration for any success I've achieved. To my sister, who graduated from Tufts University, where they apparently teach you how to survive the tsunamis of life, because she has done so with enormous grace. Her fight against MS is heroic, and the privilege of helping to care for her has been a true gift to me.

And to my husband and son, the love and the light of my life. I have been so blessed to have been loved by these two exceptional men. They are the story of my success.

STARTING OUT

ABOUT THE EDITOR

BECKI SMITH is the former executive producer of WCSH6's newsmagazine shows *207* and *Bill Green's Maine* and has a special interest in telling real stories of real people living life after school. When her son, Jake Smith, graduated from NYU's Tisch School of the Arts, Smith drew upon her own experience and her friendships with successful professionals in New England to create a collection of advice for him to take into the adult world. This very special gift was the inspiration for the book that became *Starting Out: Life Lessons for Graduates*, revised and expanded for a new generation of graduates. Smith lives with her husband in Portland, Maine and teaches writing for media at Southern Maine Community College. page VIII

ABOUT THE CONTRIBUTORS

BRIAN P. ALLEN is the artistic director and cofounder of Good Theater, where he has directed numerous plays, including *Good People*, *Next Fall*, *August Osage County*, *Bad Dates*, *Forum*, *Frost/Nixon*, *The Spitfire Grill*, *The Importance of Being Earnest*, *On Golden Pond*, *Driving Miss Daisy*, and *Into the Woods*, among others. He has also appeared in Good Theater's productions of *Side by Side by Sondheim*, *California Suite*, and *Barrymore*. His one-man show, *Blueberries, Broadway & Brian*, premiered at Good Theater, and now tours. In addition to his theatrical work, Brian has created and directed a number of symphony concerts for several Broadway stars, including Tony winner Debbie Gravitte and Tony nominees Mark Jacoby and Nancy Opel. He began his theatrical career at Maine State Music, where he served as the general manager / managing director for seven years. He is a member of the Society of Directors and Choreographers theatrical union. page 1

JOHN E. BALDACCI began his political career at twenty-three, when he was elected to the Bangor City Council. In 1982, he was elected to the Maine State Senate, where he served for twelve years. Baldacci was elected to the US House of Representatives in 1994, and reelected by wide margins in 1996, 1998, and 2000. Baldacci was elected governor of the State of Maine in 2002, and reelected in 2006. John Baldacci is currently a senior advisor, Economic Development and Government Relations, at Pierce Atwood. page 17

Former First Lady **KAREN M. BALDACCI** was appointed by Governor LePage to the Maine Library Commission. She has been a registered dietitian for the last twenty-four years, and as First Lady of Maine focused her work on quality early-care education, education issues, nutrition, wellness, family literacy, the cultural arts, and local agriculture. page 17

MARK H. C. BESSIRE is director of the Portland Museum of Art. Previously, he served as director of the Bates College Museum of Art in Lewiston, and as director of the Institute of Contemporary Art at the Maine College of Art in Portland, Maine. Mark is also a founding board member of the nonprofit organization Africa Schoolhouse, which is dedicated to building schools in rural Africa. page 50

SELMA BOTMAN is a special assistant to the chancellor of the University of Maine, focusing on expanding the systems of international education programs, recruiting foreign students, and coordinating overseas faculty exchanges. Prior to her appointment she served as president of the University of Southern Maine, and as the executive vice chancellor and university provost of the City University of New York. Botman is a specialist in modern Middle Eastern politics. page 55

AMY BOUCHARD is the founder and president of Isamax Snacks Inc. As a stay-at-home mom in 1994, Amy began baking and selling whoopie pies—known as Wicked Whoopies—to local stores. After two years baking from home, she moved to a commercial bakery, and is now baking an average of 10,000 Wicked Whoopies a day. Amy's Wicked Whoopie Pies have been featured on multiple Food Network Shows and in national magazines. She also currently sells them on the Home Shopping Network. page 1

RICH BROOKS is the founder of flyte new media, a web design and Internet branding company. He is also an expert blogger at FastCompany.com and a featured blogger at MaineBusiness.com. page 59

After graduating from Williams College, ROB CALDWELL worked as a taxi driver, bellhop, and substitute teacher. Since 1984 he has been an anchor and reporter at WCSH-TV in Portland, Maine. page 67

After being featured on both classical and punk rock records, CHRIS BROWN settled into a career at Bull Moose, an eleven-store music, movie, video game, and book store chain based in Portland, Maine. He also reviews music and movies for WCSH-6 TV in Portland. page 45

DON CAMPBELL is a singer/songwriter, composer, and multi-instrumentalist whose music is inspired by sources as diverse as the Celtic and Canadian Maritimes music of his family to Dan Fogelberg, Vince Gill, the Beatles, and novelist Stephen King. Don has released twelve CDs, most recently a two-disc, twenty-three-song collection, *Kites to Fly: Celebrating the Music of Dan Fogelberg*. Co-based in Portland, Maine, and Nashville, Tennessee, Don averages between 150 to 200 performances per year. page 19

MIKE CHITWOOD began his career in law enforcement with the Philadelphia Police Department as a patrol officer, highway patrol officer, and then a detective in the prestigious homicide division. His career later led him to serve as chief of police for Portland, Maine. In 2005, Mike returned to the Delaware Valley, as he was named superintendent of police of the Upper Darby Township Police Department. page 46

JAMES "HUEY" COLEMAN has been making films about artists, education, the environment, and Maine for thirty years. His films have been shown at film festivals throughout the United States, on PBS, and on television in Europe. He is a recipient of a fellowship in film from the Maine Arts Commission, and is a member of the Maine Touring Artists program and the New Hampshire Arts in Education Program. He is a founder of the Maine Student Film and Video Festival, and served as its director for thirty-one years. He has been an artist-in-residence in over 150 schools in New England. Currently he is an adjunct instructor in Communications and New Media, Southern Maine Community College. His latest feature-length documentary, *In Good Time, The Piano Jazz of Marian McPartland*, was released in 2011. **page 35**

JOHN COLEMAN founded The VIA Agency in 1993, and has been the Portland, Maine–based agency's CEO since then. The agency was named *Ad Age's* Small Agency of the Year in 2011, and was twice on the *Inc. 500* list of fastest-growing companies. John and the agency have tackled some of the most difficult marketing challenges in the industry, working with leading brands like Samsung, Unilever, Sam's Club, Perdue Farms, Welch's, Shutterfly, Republic Wireless, The World Trade Center, Romano's Macaroni Grill, and 1800 Tequila. **page 36**

SUSAN COLLINS, first elected Maine Senator in 1996, is serving her third term in the US Senate. Known for her work in facilitating bipartisan compromise, Senator Collins is a key leader in the US Congress. Along with former Senator Joe Lieberman, Senator Collins led the successful repeal of the discriminatory "Don't Ask, Don't Tell" law that prohibited gay and lesbian Americans from serving openly in the military. After her reelection in 2002, Senator Collins became chairman of the Homeland Security Committee. In 2004, she coauthored the Collins-Lieberman Intelligence Reform and Terrorism Prevention Act. A recipient of the Navy's highest civilian honor, Senator Collins has successfully fought for increased funding for the navy at Bath Iron Works. During her entire time in the US Senate, she has never missed a roll-call vote, casting more than five thousand consecutive votes—and counting! **page 75**

JERRY COLPITTS is an actor who has performed in shows Off Broadway and in various soap operas. In the early 1980s he worked for Marvel Comics, portraying The Amazing Spider-man at high-profile promotional events around the globe, working closely with the legendary Stan Lee. Jerry is also involved with NYU Theater and Film Departments, lending his voice to staged readings and small productions. **page 24**

ROBERT "BOB" CROWLEY was the $1,000,000 winner of the American television show *Survivor: Gabon*. At fifty-seven, he is the oldest winner in the history of *Survivor*, and he also tied the record for winning the most consecutive challenges. Bob is a retired high school physics teacher. In 2009, Crowley published his autobiography, *Making Waves: The Stories of Maine's Bob Crowley*. **page 14**

Meteorologist **JOE CUPO** has been part of the WCSH-TV *News Center* team since 1979. He forecasts each weekday for *News Center 6* at five ᴘᴍ, five-thirty ᴘᴍ, six ᴘᴍ, and eleven ᴘᴍ. Joe is an avid cyclist and a longtime spokesperson for the MS Bike Ride, which raises money to help people living with multiple sclerosis. **page 73**

BRIAN DEAN CURRAN was US Ambassador to Haiti from 2000 to 2003, where he played a prominent role in health issues. A career member of the US Foreign Service until his retirement in 2005, Curran also served in Washington, DC, Niger, Guinea-Bissau, Belgium, France, Ireland, and Mozambique, and in Italy, where he worked for NATO. Curran now serves as vice president of the board of trustees of Konbit Sante. page 16

HABIB DAGHER is a professor of civil/structural engineering at the University of Maine, Bath Iron Works Professor of Structural Engineering, and founding director of the Advanced Structures and Composites Center. The Center does contract research for private companies worldwide, as well as US government agencies. Recently, the Advanced Structures and Composites Center has received $15 million in funding from the Department of Energy for the development of offshore wind energy off Maine's coast. Dr. Dagher has received numerous awards for his work, including the University of Maine's Distinguished Maine Professor Award in 1995. He has written over 120 technical publications. page 32

PATRICK DEMPSEY is a film and television actor best known for his role on the medical series *Grey's Anatomy*, as neurosurgeon Dr. Derek Shepherd (aka "Dr. McDreamy"). He is a two-time Golden Globe nominee, and has starred in films such as *Enchanted* (2007) and *Made of Honor* (2008). Dempsey is an avid sports-car racer, having participated in the Indianapolis and Daytona Beach events. A Maine native, he established the Patrick Dempsey Center for Cancer Hope & Healing in Lewiston after his mother developed ovarian cancer. page 30

JESSE DERRIS is the founder and CEO of Derris & Company, a brand strategy and public relations firm headquartered in New York City. Before founding the firm, he served as senior vice president and partner at Sunshine Sachs, where he led the firm's work in a variety of vertical markets, including finance, crisis, digital, sports, and real estate. He began his career in politics at a boutique public relations and public affairs firm in Washington, D.C., and served as a state spokesman on John Kerry's 2004 presidential campaign. page 32

PAUL DOIRON is the author of the Mike Bowditch series of crime novels, including *The Poacher's Son*, which won the Barry Award and the Strand Critics Award for Best First Novel, and was nominated for an Edgar Award. He is editor emeritus of *Down East* magazine, having served as editor in chief from 2005 to 2013, before stepping down to write full-time. Paul is a Registered Maine Guide specializing in fly fishing and outdoor recreation. page 51

With more than thirty-five years' experience in film and television, ROB DRAPER has worked on everything from regional TV news to Hollywood feature films. Known as a technical innovator and creative risk taker in the industry, he has pioneered many new techniques, and worked on development of motion picture products for SONY, Panasonic, Fuji Film, Arri, and Zeiss. Rob was also the first to run a full-scale high-definition shoot in Hollywood on the then "new gen" cameras. Rob's photography on the Sundance Audience award-winner, *The Spitfire Grill*, drew accolades worldwide. Rob has worked on TV movies, feature films, mini series, TV series documentaries, TV commercials, and music videos for every major Hollywood studio and US TV network. More recently he has been on the cutting edge of digital technology on the web, with his groundbreaking IPTV channel, Singlemalt TV. page 61

GREG ECONOMOS is senior vice president of global consumer products for Sony Pictures Consumer Products, which oversees and manages the licensing and merchandising efforts for some of the best film and television brands in the industry. Prior to joining Sony, Economos worked at Saban Entertainment during the height of the *Power Rangers* years, and at Fox Kids and Fox Family Worldwide, overseeing business and legal affairs for its consumer products, marketing, and Internet groups. page 30

JONATHAN EDWARDS is a singer/songwriter whose highly respected repertoire includes such classics as "Honky Tonk Stardust Cowboy," "Sometimes," "One Day Closer," "Don't Cry Blue," "Emma," "Everybody Knows Her," "Athens County," and everyone's favorite ode to putting a good buzz on, "Shanty." His song "Sunshine (Go Away Today)," was first released in 1971, and almost forty years later continues to be embraced by faithful followers and new fans alike. page 74

CHARLIE ESHBACH'S baseball career began in 1974 with the Elmira Pioneers (NY-Penn League). A year later he joined the Bristol Red Sox, Boston's Double-A team in the Eastern League. Eshbach is the longest-serving active member of the Eastern League, having served as its president for eleven years. In 1988, Charlie served as interim president of Minor League Baseball. Charlie, the Sea Dogs' first employee, has been with the club since its inception in the fall of 1992. page 5

MARY ANN ESPOSITO is the creator and host of the nationally televised PBS series, *Ciao Italia with Mary Ann Esposito*, which is the longest-running cooking series in television history. Through *Ciao Italia* and appearances on other television programs, including the *Today* show, *Regis and Kelly*, QVC, the Food Network, Discovery Channel, Fox, Martha Stewart Radio, RAI International, *The Victory Garden*, *Simply Ming* (and so many others!), Mary Ann Esposito has been able to share traditional Italian cooking with audiences around the world. She is the author of twelve cookbooks, her most recent, is *Ciao Italia Family Classics*. **page 49**

TIM FERRELL is the founder of both The Comedy Workshop and Before You Speak. Tim was also a writer for Comedy Central and talent coordinator for the Who's on First comedy club, where some of his students were Jon Stewart, Chris Rock, and Ray Romano. Tim has taught workshops in Maine for beginners as well as established stand-up comedians. He describes this work as "saving the world from tedium, one speaker at a time." **page 68**

TESS GERRITSEN is an international best-selling author and physician. Her first novel was *Call After Midnight*, a romantic thriller, and was followed by eight more romantic suspense novels. She also wrote a screenplay, *Adrift*, which aired as a 1993 CBS Movie of the Week starring Kate Jackson. Tess's first medical thriller, *Harvest*, marked her debut on the *New York Times* best-seller list. Her suspense novels since then have been top-three best-sellers in the United States and abroad. Her series of novels featuring homicide detective Jane Rizzoli and medical examiner Maura Isles inspired the TNT television series *Rizzoli & Isles*, starring Angie Harmon and Sasha Alexander. **page 68**

KIM GRABINA-COMO is a producer and journalist for NBC News Partnerships, where she produces, develops, and pitches original content from NBC Network shows to NBC's two hundred–plus affiliate stations. She works closely with *Nightly News with Brian Williams*, *Dateline*, and *Today*. In addition to her full-time gig, Kim is also the cocreator of the mommy blog, 2 Moms on a Train (2momsonatrain.com), which focuses on balancing work, life, kids, and everything in between. **page 37**

LINDA GREENLAW, America's only female swordfishing captain, is author of three *New York Times* best-selling books about life as a commercial fisherman: *The Hungry Ocean*, *The Lobster Chronicles*, and *All Fishermen Are Liars*. Time magazine called her *Recipes from a Very Small Island*, coauthored with her mother, Martha Greenlaw, a "must-have cookbook." Greenlaw's latest book, *Seaworthy: A Swordfish Boat Captain Returns to the Sea*, is a chronicle of her return to swordfishing after ten years as a lobsterman. Linda was featured in the hit Discovery Channel series *Swords: Life on the Line*. She first came to the public's attention in Sebastian Junger's *The Perfect Storm*, where Junger called her "one of the best captains . . . on the entire East Coast." **page 42**

JOSIANE GRÉGOIRE is a dean at New York University, where she is director of admissions and enrollment services in NYU's Liberal Studies Program. Previously she has worked for the NAACP Legal Defense Fund. At Columbia University she was special assistant to the office of the president. **page 39**

SHANNON MOSS HAGERTY has worked in the Portland, Maine, television market since 1999, having reported and anchored news programs on WMTW and WCSH. She currently hosts and produces the online newsmagazine show, *Split Screen with Shannon Moss*. **page 67**

CAL HANCOCK spent twenty-five years as a senior executive in several medical information management companies, where she focused on customer service and quality control. Cal returned to Maine, where she combined her business experience with her love of good cooking, creating the Hancock Gourmet Lobster Company in December of 2000. In just a few short years, her company has become the market leader in high-value, gourmet lobster and seafood products. **page 3**

DAN HARRIS is the co-anchor of ABC News' weekend edition of *Good Morning America*. His other platforms have included *World News with Diane Sawyer*, *Good Morning America*, *Nightline*, ABC News Digital, and ABC News Radio. For four years Harris anchored *World News Sunday*. Prior to joining ABC News, Harris was an anchor at New England Cable News (NECN), and an anchor and political reporter at WCSH, an NBC affiliate in Portland, Maine, for two years. He began his broadcasting career as a reporter for WLBZ, the NBC affiliate in Bangor, Maine. Harris is the recipient of an Edward R. Murrow Award and an Emmy Award. **page 10**

ANGIE HELTON is the founder of Northeast Media Associates, a multimedia public relations firm. With more than eleven years of experience as a television news producer in New York, New Jersey, and Boston, Angie has been nominated for six regional Emmy Awards, winning two, and has been recognized for her outstanding media work with a national Telly Award. **page 13**

HANNAH HOLMES is an American writer, journalist, essayist, and science commentator for *Science Live* (Discovery Channel) and radio shows such as *Maine Things Considered*. She has published four books, most recently *Quirk: Brain Science Makes Sense of Your Peculiar Personality*, and various articles online and in magazines. **page 34**

GEOFF and **MICHAEL HOWE** are inventors, military contractors, actors, and entrepreneurial businessmen. The brothers first gained notoriety in 2001 with the development of the Ripsaw, an unmanned ground vehicle designed for the US military. In 2009, *Popular Science* magazine named Ripsaw MS1 "Invention of the Year," and in 2010 the *Guinness World Records* awarded Howe and Howe Tech another record-breaker as developers of the

World's Smallest Armored Vehicle, the Badger. Mike and Geoff also starred in their own reality television show titled *Black Ops Brothers: Howe and Howe Tech*, and have custom-built prop vehicles for several production companies.
page 25 (Geoff) / 46 (Michael)

JEFF INGLIS is the former managing editor of the *Portland Phoenix* and an explorer of the world through journalism, travel, reading, mindfulness, and compassion. The suggestions he makes here are also among those he strives to live by. He also encourages everyone to take risks, to push themselves, and to try new things. You never know what the world is holding out for you. page 71

In a career spanning more than half a century, Maine artist DAHLOV IPCAR has written and illustrated more than thirty children's and young adult books, starting with *The Little Fisherman* (by Margaret Wise Brown) in 1945, and including *The Cat at Night*, *One Horse Farm*, and *My Wonderful Christmas Tree*. Today, Ipcar's intricate, distinctive, and fanciful artwork is known worldwide, with pieces of her work in the collections of numerous renowned museums, including The Metropolitan Museum of Art and the Whitney Museum of American Art. Ipcar still lives and paints in the 1860s farmhouse that she has lived in for nearly seventy years. page 12

BRADFORD KENNEY is a New England–based artistic director, producer, stage director, and artist. Since joining the Ogunquit Playhouse in 2005, the Playhouse has doubled its audience, growing into one of the Northeast's pre-eminent regional theaters. Kenney is also noted for his work at Carnegie Hall including directing the holiday special, *The Christmas Rose*, starring Jane Seymour, and producing An *American Christmas Carol* with Tim Janis. page 38

RUSHWORTH KIDDER was widely known as a provocative speaker/author who focused his insights on corporate and global ethics. Dr. Kidder's book, *Moral Courage*, used real-life stories from business, education, government, sports, and other areas to explain what moral courage is, what it does, and how we can develop it. His previous book, How Good *People Make Tough Choices: Resolving the Dilemmas of Ethical Living*, has been praised by Jimmy Carter as "a thought-provoking guide to enlightened and progressive personal behavior." Dr. Kidder founded the Institute for Global Ethics in 1990. page 64

PETE KILPATRICK is an independent American singer/songwriter who has released six records independently with the Pete Kilpatrick Band. Kilpatrick's work is a blend of folk and pop rock music, and he has been named Maine's Best Act and Best Vocalist four times in the Portland Best Music Awards. Pete has toured with many notable acts, including Jason Mraz and the Dave Matthews Band. In 2012, Pete and his band performed at President Obama's only campaign stop in Maine. page 58

As both a writer and show-runner, **JEFF KLINE** has been responsible for more than forty live-action and animated series and pilots, including the multiple Daytime Emmy Award–winning *Transformers Prime* (The Hub), *That Was Then* (ABC), and a slew of venerable animated series, including *Jackie Chan Adventures* (Kids WB), *Men in Black: The Animated Series* (Kids WB), and *Dragon Tales* (PBS). In 2013, Kline formed Darby Pop Publishing, a comic book imprint distributed worldwide by IDW. page 37

ELINOR KLIVANS is a cookbook author and food writer who specializes in desserts and home baking. Home cooks have come to rely on her "bake and freeze" books to create sweet treats now to serve later. She trained as a pastry chef in France and the United States, and, before becoming a writer, worked for several years as a dessert chef. In addition to *Bake and Freeze Dessert*s, Elinor is the author of *Big Fat Cookies*, *Bake and Freeze Chocolate Desserts*, *125 Cookies to Bake, Nibble, and Savor*, and *Fearless Baking: Over 100 Desserts that Anyone Can Make*. Her most recent titles are *Cupcakes!*, *Pot Pies*, and *The Essential Chocolate Chip Cookbook*. page 24

MICHAEL LAFAVORE was the founding editor of *Men's Health* magazine and its editor in chief for twelve years. During his tenure, Lafavore also launched menshealth.com. Later, Lafavore served as general manager for the successful launch of the US edition of *The Week* at Dennis Publishing. The following year he was named editor in chief of *TV Guide* and TVGuide.com. Most recently, Lafavore was editorial director of Meredith Publishing. In 2012, Lafavore oversaw a redesign of *Maxim* magazine. Lafavore was a faculty member of the Stanford Publishing Courses for eight years, and has lectured at New York University, Columbia, and Lehigh University. He began his journalism career at daily newspapers in New England. page 50

GRETCHEN LIBBY is the executive in charge of business development and global strategy, managing and overseeing Industrial Light & Magic's client marketing and bidding efforts, strategic partnerships, and global expansion. Gretchen joined ILM in 1997 as the Sabre department production manager, producing three hundred *Star Wars: Special Edition* shots. She was promoted to visual effects producer in June 2000 on *Star Wars Episode II: Attack of the Clones*. Prior to ILM, Libby worked in visual effects film production at Pacific Data Images in Palo Alto, California, and in visual effects commercial production at both Image Design and Aoki Studios in New York City. page 31

Grammy Award-winning mastering engineer **BOB LUDWIG** began his professional career at A&R Recording as an assistant engineer working with Phil Ramone. In 1993 Bob opened his own business, *Gateway Mastering Studios, Inc.*, in Portland, Maine. Bob has mastered countless gold and platinum records. page 8

ANOUAR MAJID is the author of the novel *Si Yussef*, and five nonfiction books. He is the vice president for global affairs at the University of New England in Maine. page 13

ROBERT COCHRANE ("BOB") MARLEY JR. is an American comedian who has appeared on *Late Show with David Letterman*, *Late Night with Conan O'Brien*, and Comedy Central. He can be seen in the film, *The Boondock Saints*. Marley's comedic bits are mostly about life in Maine. He has hosted on XM Radio and, as of 2013, appears weekly on Coast 93.1-WMGX in Portland, Maine, in a segment called "The World According to Bob." In 2010 Marley entered the *Guinness World Records* with the longest continuous stand-up routine. He completed forty hours of standup comedy, the first seventeen hours and fourteen minutes without any repetition of material. Marley's record was broken by David Scott on April 30, 2013, with a time of forty hours and eight minutes. page 36

MICHAEL H. MICHAUD was sworn in as a US congressman in January 2003 to represent the Second Congressional District of Maine. Mike was elected to the Maine Legislature in 1980, and served seven terms before being elected to the State Senate in 1994. He is also a twenty-nine-year employee of Great Northern Paper. page 33

BARRY MILLS is president of Bowdoin College, where he has underscored the primacy of Bowdoin's academic program and has worked with the faculty to redefine a liberal arts education for the twenty-first century. Mills, who holds a doctorate in biology as well as a law degree, previously served as the deputy presiding partner of Debevoise & Plimpton in New York City, one of the nation's preeminent international law firms. page 3

DR. DORA ANNE MILLS practiced hospital-based pediatrics in Los Angeles for two years and spent a year volunteering in Tanzania, East Africa, before returning to practice in her hometown of Farmington, Maine. She was tapped by Governor King's administration in 1996 to serve as the director for public health for Maine, a position she held for fifteen years, and under two governors, including Governor Baldacci. She is currently vice president for clinical affairs at the University of New England. page 21

GEORGE J. MITCHELL served as US Special Envoy for Middle East Peace from January 2009 to May 2011. Prior to that he had a distinguished career in public service, having been appointed to the US Senate in 1980 to complete the unexpired term of Senator Edmund S. Muskie. He was elected to a full term in the Senate in 1982, and went on to an illustrious career in the Senate, spanning fifteen years. He left the Senate in 1995 as the Senate majority leader, a position he had held since January 1989. Mitchell also served as the Independent Chairman of the Northern Ireland Peace Talks. Under his leadership, the Good Friday Agreement—a historic accord ending decades of conflict—was agreed to by the governments of Ireland and the United Kingdom and the political parties of Northern Ireland. In 2008, *Time* magazine named Senator Mitchell one of the one hundred most influential persons in the world. **page 29**

KAREN MORGAN has appeared in comedy clubs across the country, from Caroline's in New York to the Laugh Factory in Hollywood. She began her comedy career as a finalist on Nick at Nite's *The Search for the Funniest Mom in America*. Since then, she has also been seen on NBC, Nick Jr., CBS, NESN, and Court TV. Karen brings laughter to morning commuters and radio listeners around the country, including a one-hour comedy special and clips on Sirius/XM Satellite Radio. **page 55**

EVA MURRAY moved to Matinicus Island in 1987 to teach in the one-room school. Two years later she married the island electrician and stayed to raise their family there. Over the years she has started a small bakery, become an emergency medical technician, taken on a number of roles in municipal government and volunteer organizations, started the community's recycling program, and been a first responder to emergencies both real and imagined. Since 2003 she's also been a regular columnist for several mainland publications. Eva bakes bread in a woodstove, spins wool, digs potatoes, collects useful herbs, cuts hay with a scythe, and swings a blacksmith's hammer. (Not surprisingly, she sometimes writes her articles with pencil and paper.) **page 27**

CHRISTIANE NORTHRUP, MD, is a leading authority in the field of women's health and wellness. A board-certified ob/gyn physician, she was an assistant clinical professor of ob/gyn at Maine Medical Center for twenty years. Dr. Northrup is the author of two *New York Times* best-selling books, *Women's Bodies, Women's Wisdom* and *The Wisdom of Menopause*. In 2005, *Mother-Daughter Wisdom*, her third book, was voted Amazon's number-one book of the year in both parenting and mind-body health. Dr. Northrup has hosted seven highly successfully public television specials, her latest based upon the newly revised edition of *Women's Bodies, Women's Wisdom*. Dr. Northrup has been featured on *The Oprah Winfrey Show*, the *Today* show, *NBC Nightly News*, *The View*, the *Rachael Ray Show*, *Good Morning America*, ABC's *20/20*, and *The Dr. Oz Show*. In 2013, *Reader's Digest* named her one of "The 100 Most Trusted People in America." **page 11**

HOLLY NUNAN has a blog on MaineToday.com and a podcast, Newz By The Nunz, about Maine's local music scene. She is a frequent guest on WCSH6's *The Morning Report*. **page 8**

LES OTTEN was the CEO and chairman of the board of the American Skiing Company. In 2001 he helped form New England Sports Ventures (later known as Fenway Sports Group), which purchased the Boston Red Sox and led the team to its first World Series Championship in eighty-six years, in 2004. After leaving the skiing and baseball business, Otten started Maine Energy Systems, a wood-pellet heating company. page 31

JEANNE PAQUETTE is commissioner of labor for the State of Maine. With more than twenty years' experience in human resources management, Commissioner Paquette specialized in both training and management development. She was also the founder of an industry-related media business which published the *Employment Times*, *HR Times*, and MyJobWave.com. page 61

RICHARD L. PATTENAUDE is president of Ashford University and has served as president of the University of Southern Maine and chancellor of the University of Maine System. page 64

ELIZABETH (LIZ) PEAVEY is a prizewinning writer, teacher, and performer of her one-woman show, *My Mother's Clothes Are Not My Mother*. She is the author of *Glorious Slow Going: Maine Stories of Art, Adventure and Friendship*, *Outta My Way: An Odd Life Lived Loudly*, and of *Maine & Me*. Peavey's writing has been featured in *Down East* magazine, where she is a contributing editor. Her monthly humor column, "Outta My Yard," can be found at thebollard.com. page 43

RYAN MICHAEL PETERS, better known by his stage name, *Spose*, is an American rapper from Wells, Maine. In January 2010, Spose's single, "I'm Awesome," received airplay on Maine radio stations. After the song caught on in other parts of the United States, Spose signed a record deal with Universal Republic Records. "I'm Awesome" peaked at #37 on the Billboard Hot 100. Spose's latest CD, *Dankonia*, was released in late fall of 2013, along with the *Almost Complete Lyrics Book*. page 49

Congresswoman **CHELLIE PINGREE** moved to Maine in the 1970s, and after graduating from College of the Atlantic, she and her husband started a small farm on the island of North Haven. A knitting business she started in the early 1980s soon grew to ten year-round employees producing knitting kits and books that were sold in hundreds of stores across the country. Pingree served in the Maine Senate before going on to become the national president of Common Cause. In 2008 Chellie Pingree was elected to Congress to serve Maine's 1st District. She was the first woman from this district to ever be elected to Congress. Congresswoman Pingree has been a national leader in addressing the problem of sexual assault in the military. page 10

DOUGLAS PRESTON began his career at the American Museum of Natural History in New York as an editor, writer, and finally, manager of publications. He also taught nonfiction writing at Princeton University. With Lincoln Child, he is the coauthor of the novels *Relic*, *Riptide*, *Thunderhead*, *Fever Dream*, and *Two Graves*. *Relic* was released as a motion picture by Paramount in 1997. More recently, their novel *Cold Vengeance* hit number one on both the *New York Times* and *Wall Street Journal* best-seller lists. Preston teamed up with Italian journalist Mario Spezi, and in 2008 they published a nonfiction book, *The Monster of Florence*, which spent four months on the *New York Times* best-seller list and won numerous journalism awards in both Italy and the United States. It is currently under development as a film, starring George Clooney, who will play the part of Preston. **page 23**

BILL RYAN JR. has owned and operated Oxford Plains Speedway since 1998. He is recognized as a leader in the racing industry, and was named as one of eight finalists for the 2008 33rd Annual Auto Racing Promoter of the Year Award. Prior to owning the Speedway, Bill was a marketing executive in the racing industry, and practiced law in Portland. Ryan is a member of the board of trustees of the Portland Museum of Art and the Pine Tree Council of the Boy Scouts of America. **page 5**

MIKE SACKS has written for *Vanity Fair*, *Esquire*, *GQ*, *The New Yorker*, *Time*, *New York Times*, *Washington Post*, *McSweeney's*, *Radar*, *Funny or Die*, *MAD*, *New York Observer*, *Premiere*, *Believer*, *Vice*, *Maxim*, *Women's Health*, and *Salon*. He has worked at the *Washington Post*, and is currently on the editorial staff of *Vanity Fair*. His first book, *And Here's the Kicker: Conversations with 21 Humor Writers about Their Craft*, included interviews with Buck Henry and David Sedaris. Other books by Sacks are *Sex: Our Bodies, Our Junk*, and *Your Wildest Dreams, Within Reason*. In addition, he is the co-editor of *Care to Make Love in that Gross Little Space Between Cars?*, featuring contributions from, among others, Louis C.K., Dave Eggers, Zach Galifianakis, Nick Hornby, and Weird Al Yankovic. **page 51**

TIM SAMPLE is widely acknowledged to be New England's premier native humorist. Tim's books, albums, and videos have sold well over a million copies. In the summer of 1993 Tim was recruited by Charles Kuralt to be a correspondent for the Emmy award–winning TV Show *CBS News Sunday Morning*. Over the following eleven years Tim produced over 100 "Postcards from Maine" segments, which introduced millions of CBS viewers around the nation and the world to the wonders of Tim Sample's home state. Tim averages 80 to 100 concert and after-dinner appearances per year. **page 70**

FRANCE SHEA served as director of communications for the Girl Scouts of Maine. Prior to that she worked in development for Maine PBS, and as a producer for WCBB, the PBS affiliate in Maine. page 25

ROBERT SHETTERLY'S paintings and prints are in collections all over the United States and Europe. He is well known for his series of seventy painted etchings based on William Blake's *Proverbs of Hell*. For more than ten years he has been painting the series of portraits, *Americans Who Tell the Truth*. The exhibit has been traveling around the country since 2003. The portraits have given Shetterly an opportunity to speak with children and adults all over this country about the necessity of dissent in a democracy, the obligations of citizenship, and how democracy cannot function if politicians don't tell the truth, if the media don't report it, and if the people don't demand it. page 63

PAT SIMMONS is the general manager of Cinemagic Westbrook in Maine. page 51

DR. JUDSON SMITH is a psychologist practicing in Portland, Maine. He is the former host of the shows *Kids Health* and *Kid-Wise* on WCBB, and of the series *Focus on You*, which aired on WCSH and WLBZ for ten years. He has been honored for his work as a media psychologist by the National Association of Television Program Executives and the Maine Association of Broadcasters. He is also the author of the audiobook *Every Parent Can Have Happy Kids*. page 15

OLYMPIA SNOWE is a former Republican senator from Maine. Snowe began her career in the Maine House of Representatives, served in the Maine State Senate, and was elected to the Ninety-sixth Congress, and to the seven succeeding Congresses. She was elected to the US Senate in 1994, and served until her retirement in 2012. page 57

JIM STOTT is a cofounder of Stonewall Kitchen, which he co-owns with Jonathan King. Stonewall Kitchen got its start when Jim and Jonathan began selling homemade jams at a farmers' market in Maine. Today Stonewall Kitchen is a giant in the specialty food market. Jim is also the coauthor of several cookbooks. page 41

CHAD STUART is a British singer/songwriter who was part of the folk duo, Chad and Jeremy. He wrote the classic "Yesterday's Gone." Stuart also plays piano, organ, guitar, lute, mandolin, harmonica, violin, trumpet, and the flute. page 4

NOAH TALMATCH has owned and operated six successful restaurants, a burger chain called Lucky Burger, and a famous nightclub, The Ice Bar. He has worked with chefs Alain Ducasse, Pierre Shadolin, and Cyril Renaud. He currently owns The North Point restaurant in Portland, Maine. page 11

DAVID TURIN is the executive chef and owner of David's Monument Square and Opus Ten in Portland, David's 388 in South Portland, and has been instrumental in developing David's KPT and Opus Ten in Kennebunkport. David was honored by the Maine Restaurant Association as Maine's 2012 Chef of the Year, and was recently featured in *Down East* magazine. David has owned and operated his own restaurants for nearly thirty years. When he's not in the restaurant, cooking, he can often be spotted pursuing his other passion, surfing. page 74

LOU URENECK is a professor of journalism at Boston University and the author of *Backcast and Cabin*. A former Nieman fellow, Ureneck was the deputy managing editor of the *Philadelphia Inquirer*, and his writing has appeared in numerous publications, including the *New York Times* and the *Boston Globe*. page 50

TONY V began his career as a stand-up comedian in Boston. His streetwise humor, tempered with a genuine feel for the human condition, quickly propelled him to headliner status on the national comedy club circuit, where he has worked with Jay Leno, Dennis Miller, Bobcat Goldthwait, Steven Wright, and Adam Sandler. Tony V has appeared on *Late Night with Conan O'Brien*, Comedy Central's *Tough Crowd with Colin Quinn*, and several sitcoms, including *Seinfeld* and *Boston Common*. Tony's big-screen outings include *State and Main*, *Celtic Pride*, *Housesitter*, *One Crazy Summer*, and *Shakes the Clown*, and, most recently, the blockbuster film *The Heat*, with Sandra Bullock and Melissa McCarthy. page 69

LORI VOORNAS has been a morning host on Portland, Maine, radio stations for nearly twenty years. She currently hosts the *Q97 Morning Show* with Jeff Parsons and Meredith Manning. page 46

KAREN CARBERRY WARHOLA is the director of the Maine Film Office. She has more than twenty years of hands-on production experience in the film and television industry. Karen started her television career as a camera operator at MPBN-TV. She later worked freelance for two years at Buena Vista, a division of The Walt Disney Company, before joining the staff in Burbank, CA, for an additional eight years. She later returned to the studio lot and managed Touchstone television's Prime Time Awards and their Emmy awards campaign. page 57

KATHY WHITNEY is a wife, mother, lover of nature, and all things requiring good humor. She spent twenty-two years working at L.L. Bean in communications, training, marketing, and public relations. Prior to that she owned her own restaurant, a closet-design company, managed a jazz band, and mixed drinks. She loves giving advice whether you want it or not, but never insists you take it. page 42

BRETT WICKARD grew up in Illinois and came to Maine to attend Bowdoin College. When the record store in Brunswick went out of business in the 1980s, and Brett had no summer job, he decided to open up his own record store. At the last minute he found a location, ordered some CDs with money he had saved, and Bull Moose was born. Twenty years later there are eleven Bull Moose locations in Maine and New Hampshire. Brett also runs Crickery Wood, a software development company in Portland, Maine. page 7

MARK WILCOX was the publisher/editor of *The Weekly Sentinel* and spent forty years in the newspaper business, beginning his career with the *Boston Globe*. page 56

KIRK WOLFINGER has produced and directed numerous critically acclaimed documentary programs presented nationally and internationally on all the major networks, including History Channel's *Deep Sea Detectives* and *Titanic's Final Moments: Missing Pieces*. Other recent credits include the NOVA specials, *Ancient Refuge in the Holy Land*, *To the Moon*, and *Hitler's Lost Sub*. The latter became the inspiration for the best-seller *Shadow Divers*. Wolfinger has won two Emmys and a Peabody Award. page 44

MONICA WOOD is the author of *When We Were the Kennedys: A Memoir from Mexico, Maine*, a New England best-seller, number-one best-seller in Maine, *Oprah* magazine summer-reading pick, and winner of the 2012 May Sarton Memoir Award and the Maine Literary Award. She is also the author of four works of fiction. Her widely anthologized short stories have won a Pushcart Prize, and her nonfiction has appeared in *Oprah*, the *New York Times*, *Martha Stewart Living*, and *Parade*, among others. page 56